What to Do Until

Love

Finds You

michelle mckinney hammond

HARVEST HOUSE PUBLISHERS

EUGENE, OREGON

Cover by Koechel Peterson & Associates, Minneapolis, Minnesota.

WHAT TO DO UNTIL LOVE FINDS YOU

Copyright © 1997 by Michelle McKinney-Hammond
Published by Harvest House Publishers
Eugene, Oregon 97402
www.harvesthousepublishing.com

McKinney-Hammond, Michelle, 1957–
    What to do until love finds you / Michelle McKinney-Hammond.
     p. cm.
    ISBN-13: 978-0-7369-1718-6
    ISBN-10: 0-7369-1718-7
    1. Single people—Religious life. 2. Single people—Conduct of life. 3. Christian women—Conduct of life. 4. Man-woman relationships—Religious aspects—Christianity. 6. Mate selection—Religious aspects—Christianity. I. Title.
    BV4596.S5M35 1997
    248.8'432–DC20   96-41550
                                        CIP

Printed in the United States of America

    06 07 08 09 10 11 12 13 / DP / 10 9 8 7 6 5 4 3 2

To my eternal husband
and the true lover of my soul,
JESUS CHRIST

To my parents:
William and Norma McKinney, and
George and Charity Hammond

To my wonderful sisters:
Nicole, Ayodele, Annette, Jacqueline,
Karen, Yaaba, and Anna

ACKNOWLEDGMENTS

To Alda Denise Mitchell, my patient confidante, who tried to tell me, then let me learn the hard way.

To Philomina "Bunny" Wilson, my friend and wonderful example, who challenged me to do this.

To Karen McDonald, my precious "bud," who, quite literally, made me finish what I had started.

To my sister, Nicole Neal, who cleaned up my grammatical faux pas.

To my editor, Lela Gilbert, who made me feel like a "for real" writer.

To all my loving sisters in Christ, too many to name, for all their enthusiastic encouragement.

To Bill Jensen, who caught the vision and ran with it, I offer a very sincere and inexpressible thank you.

Your love and support have humbled me.

CONTENTS

INTRODUCTION

Someone once said, "Men are like buses—you miss one, there's always another." I don't think that remark has any particular scriptural basis, but it does trigger another train of thought (no pun intended): We have to wait for the bus to come.

Now there is more than one way to wait. You can passively wait—and perhaps miss the bus because you weren't prepared to get on. Or you can actively wait—poised at the curb with all your packages balanced, ready to make the leap when the bus arrives. *How* you wait is up to you. Are you waiting in doubt and resignation? Or are you waiting in anticipation of your mate's arrival? Who sits down on the bench when they think the bus is coming?

If you're sitting down on the job, it's time for you to get up. You can do a lot to prepare your heart, your soul, your head, your everything for a mate. He could be here any minute!

In one of His parables, Jesus says we are to "occupy until He comes." By this, He means that we need to be actively and productively waiting for His return. And preparing ourselves for the day when we'll meet Him face-to-face can be exciting and fulfilling! In Psalm 37:4, we are told: "Delight thyself also in the Lord; and he shall give thee the desires of thine heart."

This same "occupying" also applies to waiting for a mate. If you are like many single women, the desire of your heart is for a husband. In fact, if you're reading this book, I assume that's true of you. If your longing is based on what *God's* desire is for you, then God has a man for you. Where he is and why he is taking so long, I don't know. But that doesn't mean he's not on his way.

Meanwhile, like I said, there's more than one way to wait...

1
The Gift

For years I walked in adamant denial of my singleness. I refused to attend "singles" events, read "singles" books, or accept the apostle Paul's rationale that we should all be single crusaders for Christ. After much discussion (I came to call them moan sessions) with my other Christian sisters, I was forced to ponder another question: Was I the unsuspecting recipient of "the gift"? "The gift" was the capacity to walk through life being totally sublime and undisturbed about one's marital status. Those possessing "the gift" were busy being concerned with spiritual things. They had spiritual battles to fight, Scriptures to explore, unsaved souls to conquer!

Of course I was concerned about spiritual things. I devoured Scriptures, and, yes, I was even actively involved in winning souls for Christ. But there was still an undeniable void in my life. I decided that the answer, for me, was no. I was waiting for God to give me the desire of my heart, and I was not going to try to beat myself into submission to a "gift" I had not been given. I felt that I had been created to be a part of someone else's life, and no how-to-be-happy-and-single manual was going to remove my frustration over "my other half's late arrival."

Learning to Listen

"You're not ready," all my married friends said. "Yes I am," I angrily answered, and proceeded to career through one painful relationship after another. My diligent search for my mate led me into dangerous territory: the land of compromise. Against the warnings of my friends, I decided I could probably convert one of those handsome, witty, unsaved men I knew and be done with it. But after emerging bloodied and discouraged, from what I decided was my last traumatic romance, I waved the white flag of surrender. I sat down at the feet of Jesus, finally ready to hear what He had to say.

To my relief He agreed that I did not have "the gift." However, He enabled me to see that I had a lot to learn before He could send me into the arms of the man He had designed me for. He encouraged me to begin my preparation by studying the Old Testament heroine Esther. As I studied, to my surprise I learned that there was a time of preparation, 12 months to be exact, before Esther's king would even see his potential bride-to-be in order to determine whether or not he wanted her to be his wife! Those 365 days were called the days of beautification. There were six months of treatments with oils, then six more months with spices and cosmetics before Esther was ready for her unveiling. Meanwhile, she was receiving instructions on how to please the king.

Of course I spiritualized all this information. "How wonderfully significant," I thought. "First, we have to be submerged in the Holy Spirit, and the fruit of the Spirit has to be operating fully in our lives, thus creating a sweet-smelling aroma in the nostrils of God! (Ah, the smell of it!) And our outward countenance should radiate our holiness!"

But there was one fact I could not spiritualize. Esther chose to take the advice of the eunuch who was in charge of all the king's women. Now I had long since worn out my closest married friend in this area. I absorbed all her advice with untiring relish, and just as quickly discarded it to carry out my own whims. After all, what did married people know? Well, Esther listened, and Esther got what she wanted. I decided to take the hint.

In Search of the Right Role

I also studied another Old Testament book—this time about a woman called Ruth. Ruth was one cool cucumber. She set her mind on the business of gleaning the fields. And by following her mother-in-law's advice (there's that word again), Ruth got her man. Ruth knew some things about submission that I had yet to learn. She was not ashamed to make her needs known, but she was acutely aware that timing was everything. I suspect she learned the importance of a quiet spirit while watching her mother-in-law deal with her husband and sons in the land of Moab.

I have to admit I initially spiritualized this story, too. "Oh, how marvelous," I sighed. "What a poetic way of portraying being caught up in the Word, and being busy about the work of harvesting souls for Christ! While I'm busy doing God's work, my husband will notice me from a distance, become intrigued, and this overwhelming desire to protect and care for me will come over him and—voila!—'victory, victory will be mine.' I'll be married in no time!" As time passed, however, I learned that these timeless stories contained far more than spiritual lessons. I'll share some of their practical wisdom with you in the pages that follow.

Gradually as I studied, listened to others, and sat at the feet of Jesus, I came to accept that there were certain principles that have to be followed in the course of courtship. This is not because love is a game, but because God has designed a certain role for women and a certain role for men. Now for all you women's libbers, I am not referring to becoming dishwashers and doormats. But I am convinced that the only way to have an effective relationship—the way God has designed it—is for both parties to stick to their roles.

Imagine attending a play only to find that the leading man decided to take over the leading lady's lines or vice versa. The audience would become confused and the play's flow would be destroyed. Theater reviewers often take the time to analyze whether or not an actor or actress is suitable for a role, and what effect their portrayal has on the overall feel of the movie or play. Roles are very important and not easily mastered.

When I was involved in theater, there was a popular saying, "There are no small parts, only small actors." A woman's role is no smaller than a man's role. It requires just as much strength of character to be a woman as it does to be a man—and sometimes more. Each person has a responsibility to operate in his or her role in a manner that glorifies God. If this does not occur in a relationship, we sense in our spirits that something is wrong even if we aren't able to identify the problem intellectually. The results are doubt, mistrust, disrespect, lack of sensitivity to each other's needs, and eventually the demise of the relationship.

The answer to finding the right role with the right leading man in the right play is important. But it isn't as colossal a problem as it might seem at first. Through my time of listening and learning, I've discovered that we single women need to relax. We are members of a "do" society. We are programmed to "do" in order to attain. But as women of God we are called to "be." That's cause for rejoicing! It makes our lives a lot easier than we might naturally imagine.

Along the way, I've learned some valuable lessons about waiting, and I hope you'll take my advice more readily than I've sometimes taken the advice of others. If you do, I think you'll find your own days of waiting to be joyful and exciting ones.

2
First Encounters

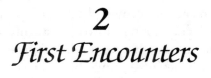

Okay, picture this scenario: Man strolls nonchalantly into room and positions himself stage left. Beautiful woman walks in moments later, accompanied by friend. They are in deep conversation. Somewhere, with her friend's story in mid-sentence, the beautiful woman's eyes shift. Cut to man across the room. He turns and his eyes lock on this incredible vision of loveliness. Everything turns to soft focus as strains of "Love Is a Many Splendored Thing" filter through the air. The words of the woman's friend echo away to nothing. All we see are her lips moving, and the look of rapture on the faces of this man and woman. They are suspended in time. He's never seen anyone as beautiful as she is. She's never felt this way before. They're in love! It must be God . . .

Cut! Cut! Cut!

I don't want to ruin your favorite romantic vision, but this kind of scene only happens in the movies. It's important to dispel myths and fantasies because being in touch with reality is essential—reality is the basis of every aspect of a relationship. Yet the media has trained us to have a lot of false ideas about what we can expect in the course of romance.

God's Love List

First of all, people do not "fall in love." Think about God's idea of love: "It is patient, kind, not jealous, doesn't brag, is not arrogant, doesn't act unbecomingly, does not seek its own, is not easily provoked, does not take into account any wrongs suffered, does not rejoice in unrighteousness but rejoices in the truth. It bears all things, believes all things, hopes all things, and endures all things. Love never fails!" (See 1 Corinthians 13:4-8.)

How can anyone "fall" into all of that? God's description of love is a definition of His own character! Love and God are synonymous—and we don't fall into God. We reach upward; we ascend to God. He, in turn, descends and comes to dwell within us.

Now picture a rose. It starts with a seed. It pushes through the soil, and grows upward. A tight little bud appears. In the fullness of time, with the right nourishment and care, the bud comes into full bloom and opens. The aroma fills the air, and we can't resist the urge to lean toward it and totally experience the incredible fragrance.

Love is like that. It starts as a small seed that presses its way through the soil (I like to think of the soil as self) to the surface, where it braves the elements. That's a very vulnerable place. The elements are things capable of destroying love— misfortunes, misunderstandings, separations, and so on.

If we refer back to God's love list, we come to the conclusion that true love is able to stand, even in the most adverse conditions. Something very special begins to happen once our hearts have been put to the test and we have survived the worst of circumstances. We bloom, we blossom, we bring forth fruit. We unfold until love cannot be contained within ourselves! It pushes to the surface; it affects everyone around us. People know when we're in love because love radiates. It fills the air with its sweet perfume.

Maybe you're thinking, "Enough already, cut to the chase. Get to the good part." Sorry, but instant gratification is not the ticket here. We're talking about laying a foundation that is going to last a lifetime. That's why it is so important to keep two little words in mind: *Slow down!*

Protecting Our Hearts

What is it about us? A man says hello and immediately we start planning our trousseau. We get all our friends involved in a relationship we've determined will take place, and then become sorely disappointed and embarrassed when things don't work out. When you meet a woman friend, do you start planning all the activities you're going to do together for the next ten years? I didn't think so. Most people realize it takes time to establish a real friendship; it takes time to know if you're compatible.

The Bible tells us to "keep our hearts with all diligence, for out of it flow the issues of life and death" (Proverbs 4:23). But how do you keep your heart when you so desperately want to give it away? We need to understand just how important and valuable our hearts really are. They require special protection—when our heart suffers, our whole being suffers. The Bible tells us in many ways how the condition of our hearts affects our health and our ability to function. God knows that the root of our heart problems is disappointment: "Hope deferred makes the heart sick" (Proverbs 13:12). That's why He suggests we be careful about what we subject our hearts to.

Let's envision another scenario: You meet a man. He's handsome; you're witty. This could work. He asks you out, you say yes. You spend the money you should be using to pay your bills to get your hair done. Then you find the ultimate dress that will make him gasp and beg for your hand in marriage—even before you can order your appetizers. You inform all your friends that tonight's the night. You compile advice, adjust your shoulder pads, and prepare for the big evening.

Love Taps

At last, there is a knock on the door. The world stops. What does that knock mean to your heart? I believe the dialogue would go something like this:

Here I stand
at the door
of your heart—your home . . .
for you see
I understand
that your heart
is where you really live . . .
will you allow me in
and let me decorate it
with love?
allow me
to throw open
the windows of your heart
and let the rooms be filled
with the fragrance of joy . . .
allow me
to place
a menagerie
of your dreams come true
upon the fragile glass shelves
of your emotions
I promise to dust them with tenderness
and to protect them
from being broken . . .
will you allow me
to hang visions of eternity
carefully framed in fulfillment
on your walls?
high . . .
where they can be
easily admired?

you see . . .
> *if I had my way*
>> *I would furnish the rooms*
>>> *with warm embraces,*
>>>> *gentle reassurances*
>>>> *and understanding*
>>> *sturdily built*
> *to endure the test of time and wear . . .*
>> *and the floors . . .*
>>> *the floors would be*
>>>> *covered with trust . . .*
>>> *the walls*
>>> *would be a beautiful hue of patience*
>> *and the light of hope*
would illuminate
> *every dark corner*
>> *and cast prisms of unselfishness*
>>> *upon the mirrors that would reflect*
>>>> *our commitment*
>>>> *to decorate each other*
>>>>> *with love . . .*
>>>> *well . . .*
>>> *here I stand . . .*
>> *will you let me in?*

Wow! That's some knock! It certainly covers all the things a woman would be looking for. But can one person really do all those things? It's wonderful to have such high hopes, but how realistic are they? Deep inside all Christians reality lives in the form of the Holy Spirit. We can listen to Him, or we can decide to ignore Him. In the midst of all the excitement, His still, small voice sometimes gets drowned out by the clamoring of our hearts, and by our response to that knock—

You knock
> *and I stand paralyzed*
>> *blood rushing through my veins*

racing with the pounding of my heart
you knock again
and still I hesitate
trying to decide
if I'm really ready
to open that door
and let you in . . .
I catch my reflection in the mirror
and nervously I
smooth the same imaginary strand of hair
that I've been smoothing
for the last hour . . .
you see
I want to be perfect for you . . .
a third persistent knock
breaks the trance
of my preoccupation . . .
"coming," I say
not moving
afraid of letting you go
afraid of letting you in
I rely on that one word
to buy me a little more time . . .
a little more time
to subdue my emotions
dismiss my anxiety
and humor my curiosity . . .
strangely enough
a picture of mama's lemon meringue pie
comes to mind
I remember how fluffy and sweet
and inviting it looked on the outside
and how tart
it always was on the inside
a bit too bitter for my taste
and I wonder
if your love is like that . . .

so I square my shoulders
reinforce the wall around my heart
and prepare myself for disappointment
bravely deciding that anything else
would be a pleasant surprise . . .
I smooth my hair again
and adjust my smile . . .
inviting
but with just a touch of distance . . .
oh, and a smidgen of nonchalance
in reserve
for masking secret pain
should you choose to walk away . . .
you see, I'll smile
even if it kills me
so, with facade intact
resolve tightly in place
I open the door . . .
and step into your eyes . . .
eternity passes . . .
while my defenses crumble . . .
and reason vanishes . . .
leaving me to shiver in my nakedness
"do you mind if I come in?"
you ask . . .
"not at all"
I hear myself reply
"not at all"

Oh, such heavy drama! And just think—you aren't even
sure if you like him yet! Yeah, I know. You *think* you like him.
After all, he dresses nice, has a good job, says something that
vaguely alludes to his having a relationship with God, *and he
likes you!* What else could you possibly hope for? What could
possibly be wrong? It *feels* right. The Holy Spirit will agree with
me later, you say, and off you go to the races. You're looking

absolutely ravishing, and he's spouting all the things you ever wanted to hear.

One Man Who Truly Loves

Most of us women want to believe everything a man tells us because we are hoping he is "the one." So we listen, then shape our own reality. You know the one I'm talking about, the one with that trousseau you were considering earlier in the chapter. But there's one small problem: There is another reality—God's reality—in the form of the Holy Spirit. Remember Him?

Of course, you don't usually feel like agreeing with His viewpoint during your dinner date, even though He has a bird's-eye view of the situation. In spite of all His yellow-caution-flag waving during the dinner discussion, you decide that this man is the one. It really doesn't matter that you don't agree with him on several major issues, or that he sucks his teeth. He's so sweet!

Still the yellow flag waves somewhere in your peripheral vision. But how do you slow down your heart rate long enough to look with objective eyes and clarity of thought at the man who stands before you? How do you become willing to take your cues from the Holy Spirit instead of from your feelings or your biological clock?

The answers are found in another man. This man has the same line, but He has a completely different method of operation because He means what He says. He says, "Behold, I stand at the door, and knock: if any [woman] hear my voice, and open the door, I will come in to [her] and will sup with [her], and [she] with me" (Revelation 3:20). This means you can look forward to spending some quality time! This man is a wonderful conversationalist. He is tender, compassionate, warm, loving, consistent, generous, a good listener, and a wonderful friend. He is fascinating, and he knows how to treat a woman. When he promises to do "exceeding abundantly above all that [you] ask or think," look out! You are in for the thrill of a lifetime. The best part of all is that He will never leave you or forsake you.

The man I refer to is Jesus. Now don't start groaning, hear me out. I promise I am not going to give you the Jesus-is-your-husband lecture. I've heard it too, and probably cringed as much as you have. I have all the comebacks memorized—"I want a family before the rapture"; "Jesus isn't enough"; "I have physical needs." Proverbs 27:7 says, "A satisfied soul loathes the honey-comb, but to a hungry soul every bitter thing is sweet." Let me illustrate. Have you ever said, "Boy, am I starving!" and then proceeded to eat everything in sight that you knew wasn't good for you because you couldn't wait to either cook or get to a decent meal? And so it goes with men. If we focus and concentrate on the man-size hole in our hearts, it begins to take on gigantic pro-portions that threaten to consume us—along with every rational thought we might possess. This is when desperate women start to settle for men who should never be considered (much to the horror of our friends and families).

Depending on where your relationship is with Jesus, your attitude about having a mate will tend to fluctuate from des-peration to quiet acceptance of God's timing. Jesus knows how you feel. He knows you have physical needs. But please know this: Since we are part of a royal harem (as I like to think of it, although we jointly make up the singular bride of Christ), we don't have to settle for less than the best. Jesus has no inten-tion of entrusting us to the care of spiritual paupers who are incapable of recognizing our true worth. (We'll talk about that later.)

Intimacy with the King of Love

So how do we move the meter from desperation and unrest to regal serenity? Let's take a deeper look at our relationship with Jesus and talk about being in love with Him. When Jesus knocked on the door of your heart and you let Him in, did you assign Him a seat in your living room and leave Him there? Did you feel you had done your duty by dubbing Him "your personal Lord and Savior"—and that's quite enough, thank you? Or did you decide to have a *real* relationship with Him?

Jesus wants to see your whole life. He wants to see what your bedroom looks like (that's a whole chapter by itself!). He wants to see the kitchen, too, and He has a couple of suggestions to make about your eating utensils and your diet. And how about the bathroom? He wants to give you a new perfume called "Fruit of the Spirit." He wants the two of you to be so close that He can freely roam around and make Himself at home in your private world. But He also respects your space; He is not going to move off that couch until you ask.

How's your conversation with Jesus? Is it an even exchange or is it boring, formal, impersonal, and one-sided? Jesus wants to sit on the floor, share popcorn, and discuss your day. He wants to talk about what you like and don't like, what makes you laugh, cry, or sigh. He wants to discuss the argument you had with your boss today. He wants to help you decide what you should wear tomorrow. He wants to have a real dialogue with you. He is interested in every little thing about you!

Isn't that what you've been looking for?

Jesus isn't too weary to have midnight conversations when you can't sleep. He doesn't even mind sitting on the toilet and keeping you company while you take your bath. Come on now— I'm talking about real intimacy! The kind you would (or should) have with a physical husband. How can you master real intimacy if you haven't practiced it? You can learn all about it with Jesus and not have to suffer the fear of rejection.

I have a friend who was one of the happiest, self-satisfied single people I know. (Notice I said *was*, she's married now.) She told me once that she practiced the presence of Christ constantly, to the extent that even when she got into her car she would say, "Come on, Jesus, put on Your seatbelt, we're getting ready to go." That might sound silly to some of you, but it is a simple gesture that can make His existence more real to you.

As you begin experiencing the presence of Jesus, several things will begin to happen: You won't focus on being alone as much; you will begin to feel loved and cherished; and the more you delight yourself with the Lord, the more He'll arrange pleasant little surprises to show you how delighted He is with you. He's promised to do so. "Delight yourself also in the LORD, and He shall give you the desires of your heart" (Psalm 37:4). Remember, He knows what you like, and He is a giver.

Jesus is the model man. He is not afraid of commitment, He has no problems with intimacy, and He is more than ready to have a deep, lasting relationship with you. Relationships are His specialty. He *created* romance. He knows how it should work. In fact, once you've experienced a truly intimate relationship with Him, you'll notice something happening to your standards as you look at the men around you. You will have more aware-ness about how you should be treated, so you'll start comparing ordinary men to Jesus! Of course they cannot be Jesus, but you can come up with a list of realistic criteria, now that you have a reference point.

Once you find intimacy with Jesus, you'll be able to slow down enough to check out the qualities of the men you meet. You'll be more willing to listen to what the Holy Spirit has to say about your date, regardless of his dashing appearance. You will become more discriminating and waste less time wading through the debris of many hopeless relationships and hurtful experiences.

So now you are developing this wonderful relationship with Jesus. You're learning about intimacy firsthand. You've reached that place of feeling good about where you are. . . . And then you meet this man. The Holy Spirit seems to have given His stamp of approval. Now what? Please don't start champing at the bit! Remember, you are already a well-kept woman, a woman of God.

Let's move on to the intricacies of a relationship with a human male, beginning with the challenging issue of physical intimacy.

3
The Intimate Challenge

"Physical intimacy!" you exclaim. "Oh no, why do you have to bring that up so soon? I was just getting comfortable."

Well, like it or not, "soon" is about the time the subject of sex usually comes up. It happens as soon as we've become emotionally relaxed. Let's turn our imaginations back to our internal movie screens. Remember the date we envisioned in the last chapter? Now we'll pick up where we left off.

Like a Moth to a Flame

I believe you were at dinner. You've eaten, you've talked, you've laughed, and now you're standing at your front door. You coyly say you've had a wonderful evening and turn to go inside, but on second thought . . . he's *so* cute, why not let him in for awhile. Ooo . . .

Tensions build inwardly, but you're cool. You are the "hostess with the mostest." You offer him coffee, tea, or Kool-aid, and take your places on the couch.

In the midst of a perfectly innocent conversation you begin to relax. "There," you say to yourself, "I told you nothing would happen."

About that time, boyfriend has noted your relaxed state and moves in with strategy tactic number one. It's called the I-want-you-to-be-totally-comfortable-with-me (in other words, "trust me") conversation. It goes something like this:

From the moment I saw you
   I felt I knew you
     in the spirit
       and out . . .
       and I was drawn like a moth to a flame
   to your eyes
  longing to look
    into the windows of your soul
  and touch the one who
    peeked surreptitiously
  through the drawn curtains
    of a mysterious smile
      that fought to reveal nothing
        but told me enough . . .
 told me of past hurts
  and tears in the night
    of unexpressed longings
      and deep disappointments
      of ambivalent hopes
    for a better tomorrow . . .
and silent questions held captive in the heart
  for God
    and God alone
and yet I wanted to answer them
   to fill the empty spaces in your soul . . .
    to stroke your hair
knowing there was more for me to know
  and explore in the heart of you
    I decided to render myself
      a peace offering
    in exchange for your trust . . .
      to wait

> *for your invitation*
> *to visit the places in you*
> *that you've so*
> *diligently protected*
> *from prying eyes*
> *and insincere questions . . .*
> *while holding fast to my confession*
> *that in some*
> *unspoken measure*
> *I know you*
> *and still I am challenged*
> *to search your soul more deeply*
> *to know even more*
> *and in the knowing*
> *learn of how*
> *to love you completely . . .*

"Oh Lord, please have mercy on my quivering soul!" you're thinking about now. And justifiably so. How can you not give in to all that! Here is a man who wants to know you *and* love you in return. Something is telling you not to let this one get away! This is when many seemingly intelligent women begin making foolish choices.

How Far Is Too Far?

The world has somehow gotten us to believe that the way to a man's heart is through his body. But the bigger lie is buried in the center of that statement because it implies that we women have nothing else to offer except our bodies. When we allow this subtle lie of Satan to influence our reasoning, we become victims of a double-edged deception. If our bodies are all we have to offer, we're in trouble. Unless we're Olympic gold medalists in the bedroom (and who knows what really constitutes that), we stand to lose based on expectations we don't even know about. Being the world's greatest lover is purely subjective.

God never meant for us to have to bear that kind of pressure. Sex was designed to be a response to love, not a foundation for it. It was to be the cement and seal of an already established commitment made in the presence of witnesses who stood in agreement before God. If we settle for conditions less than this, we leave ourselves open for pain and, in some cases, irreparable damage.

"But you don't understand!" you say. "You don't know how long it's been." "You can't possibly imagine how good it feels to be caressed, and kissed, and held, and . . . well, you know." Oh, I know all right. I've been there. I have tried to dance on the thin edge of temptation, only to fall.

Believe me, trial and error is not the best way to test God's Word because, when you least expect it, an explosion *will* occur. I've been there, done that too. If you're all wondering if I'm really saved, let me assure you, I am. But I'm also human enough to realize that most of you reading this book have not yet ascended to lofty heights of spirituality where your flesh and its longings are no longer an issue.

Christian women, including me and you, have been in places where we've wondered how much is too much. We have run the gamut from "one kiss won't hurt" to "how far can I go without totally compromising my faith and feeling guilty about it later?" Some of us have even rationalized and spiritualized oral sex so that it is permissible for easing tension until you can move on to intercourse. Come on now! Don't cringe and pretend you don't know anything about this. I am being brazenly honest because Satan does his best damage by cloaking his victims in secrecy. These things need to be brought out in the open and dealt with—it's the only road to victory.

If you've found yourself in any of the above-mentioned situations, don't beat yourself to death—but don't stay there either. Get up, repent, dust yourself off, and move on. You aren't the only one who's fallen short, regardless of what the devil is telling you. And yes, God will forgive you. He sees your heart, and He's willing to walk with you and work with you until you get it right.

And in case you've decided that you "have needs" and persist in experimenting with how far you can go before you cross the technical line, let me share with you what God told me: "You are not a store sample. The man I have chosen for you will be willing to pay the price to take you home. There is no need for a "taste test" beforehand. You are not a K-Mart blue-light special; you are a well-kept woman."

The Lord showed me that a well-kept woman is always mindful of her worth; she never stoops to being common and cheap. This woman will not be handled, examined, and thrown back into anyone's bin!

And there was one more thing—it went something like this: "You are a Tiffany diamond, and when I'm finished with you, you will be of the highest grade. No flaws. No inclusions." It takes a discriminating eye to tell the difference between a cubic zirconia and a real diamond. To put it another way, don't cast your pearls before the swine, honey. I became a woman with a new attitude based on that input from the Holy Spirit.

Not too many people have the nerve to go into Tiffany's "just looking." They respect the name, they are aware of the quality and price, so if they're not serious, they seldom move past the window. God says we should be regarded in the same light. His Word says, "Who can find a virtuous woman, her price is far above rubies" (Proverbs 31:10 KJV). God says we are so valuable that a man should be willing to pay a lifetime for us, with interest! Personally, I like the sound of that payment plan.

I realize this train of thought doesn't exactly line up with worldly thinking. But let's face it, we've been called to march to the beat of a different drummer (for our own protection, I might add).

Bible Stories for Adults Only

The Bible clearly shows that even back in the good old days, premarital sex bore serious consequences and unhappy endings for the parties involved. The first example is found in Genesis, chapter 34. It's the story of Dinah, the daughter of Jacob, and a

Hivite named Shechem. Shechem saw Miss Dinah, decided he liked what he saw, and, being the son of the ruler of the area, reasoned that he was entitled to have what he liked. So he raped her. Now this could have had a positive ending because after he committed this dastardly deed, he decided he was really in love with her and asked his father to secure her for his bride.

Well, wouldn't you know that by now the story of his premature passion had reached Dinah's brothers and father. Needless to say, they were not pleased with the news. When Shechem's father arrived to strike a deal for the hand of Dinah, the brothers made the circumcision of every man in the region part of the package. Shechem and his father willingly agreed and dashed off to convince the rest of the men in the area to cooperate. After all, they were about to acquire some very rich in-laws!

But while all the local boys were still in pain and disabled by their circumcisions, Dinah's brothers took revenge. They killed every male in the city. After reclaiming their sister, they also plundered every house and took away every flock, herd, woman, child, and article of wealth from the city and surrounding fields. That's what happens when you mess with little sister!

I suppose it is safe to assume two things in summation of this story: Jacob and his family had to get out of Dodge quick before further trouble broke out; and Dinah remained single for the rest of her life because she was no longer a virgin. Although this story is about rape, not voluntary sex, it certainly demonstrates how precious virginity was—and is—to God and His people.

Was It Love or Lust?

The next example can be found in 2 Samuel, chapter 13. Amnon, the son of David, fell in love with his step-sister Tamar (the sister of David's son Absalom). The Bible says Amnon became frustrated to the point of illness over Miss Tamar! (I think that I've-got-to-have-it love ran in the family, don't you?) Anyway, Amnon had this scheming cousin by the name of Jonadab who got sick of seeing his buddy looking down in the mouth over this woman. He concocted a scheme that would have even shocked Glenn Close's character in *Dangerous Liaisons*!

Amnon was to pretend he was ill. When his father, David, came to see him, Amnon was to request that the king send Tamar to prepare some food for him. Well, what loving father could refuse such an innocent request? So Tamar was sent for. She came and dutifully prepared Amnon's meal. When it was ready, Amnon announced that he wanted to eat in his bedchambers. He ordered everyone out of the room with the exception of Tamar.

When Tamar drew near to feed him, he grabbed her. He passionately pressed her to sleep with him. She protested, desperately trying to remind him that she would be disgraced. Why not talk to the king and ask him for her hand in marriage? Sadly, all her appeals fell on deaf ears. He raped her.

Now Mosaic law states that if a man rapes a virgin, he is to pay her father 50 shekels of silver, marry her, and never divorce her as long as she lives. Unfortunately for Tamar, once Amnon had his way with her, the Bible states, he hated her with an intense hatred. In fact, he hated her more than he had "loved" her. Despite her pleading, Amnon had her thrown out and the door bolted after her. Tamar returned home, broken and disgraced.

When Absalom, Tamar's brother, got wind of the situation, he quietly tucked the information under his hat and gently reassured Tamar not to worry her pretty little head about a thing. He waited two whole years before he struck back. How's that for controlling your temper? Absalom decided to have a banquet and invite all of his brothers, including Amnon. When Amnon was full of wine and at the height of enjoying himself, Absalom's servants struck and killed him per their master's instructions. As for Absalom, he went into self-imposed exile for three years.

And Tamar? Oh well, another virgin bites the dust.

I have to say that, in some ways, these two stories take on shades of a modern-day drama. Again, rape isn't the same as consensual sex, but there's still a connection.

"Well, I don't get it," you say. "What does all of this mean? What's the point?"

Okay, okay, I'm getting there. I want to make my point absolutely clear. Let's look at Dinah and Shechem. Someone may think, "Yes, he raped her, but he decided he loved her and wanted to marry her. What's wrong with that?" I'll tell you what's wrong with that! What was the basis for his "love"?

"Well . . . she looked fabulous!"

Okay, what else?

"I don't know."

The only two things the story tells us about Dinah are that she was pretty, and her family had lots of money. Neither one of those is enough to form the foundation of a lasting marriage. So, we can safely say that this whole situation got off to a bad start due to unclean motives. Then follow that up with distrust. And distrust, more often than not, breeds deception, which usually leads to the death of a relationship.

Dinah's brothers were not having any of it. They were not willing to allow their sister to be treated like a cheap prostitute.

Tamar and Amnon's situation hits closest to home in its relevance to modern-day society. This scenario is played out time and time again, sometimes blatantly, sometimes on a more subtle note. Amnon just had to have Tamar, and he was just going to roll over and die if he didn't get to sample the wares. Puh-leeze! It's time we looked at the facts of desire and control.

The Facts Versus the Myth

We've heard it since high school. Those pimply faced young boys would look at us in absolute pain and inform us poor little naive girls that they would be left to writhe in agony if we didn't give up our bodies. Luckily, for most of us, the fear of God (and of our mothers finding out!) overrode their agony. As for the unfortunate few who bought a young man's story, they suffered the disgrace of being labeled "easy," and, sometimes, the even more overwhelming predicament of teenage pregnancy.

Somewhere along the line, society bought into the myth that males are different, that they are not able to control their sexual needs as well as women. Notice I said *myth*. If this lack of control were the case, I believe God would have included a clause in His Word excluding men from the laws dealing with abstinence and fornication. But, since God promises not to put more on us than we can bear, I venture to say that men are not the victims of their sexuality they claim to be. The only difference between men and women in this area is that little girls are taught to control their sexual urges and behave like ladies, while boys have been taught that numerous sexual conquests are a validation of manhood.

Have you ever had a conversation with a girlfriend that went something like this? "You know, I've been out with Brian four times, and he hasn't even tried to kiss me goodnight. I thought he really liked me, but maybe he's gay." Why do we reason like that? Could it be that Brian is a man who actually wants to take it slow and get to know the real you before he decides if he wants to move in the direction of a serious relationship? Think about it.

Okay, back to Tamar and Amnon. A couple of things strike me here. First, I wouldn't doubt that Tamar actually had a crush on Amnon. She was quick to suggest that they get married. But Amnon only wanted what he wanted; he had no intention of marrying her. Her needs were not important to him—which is totally contrary to what love is all about. He was really *in lust* with her. So he raped her, and his so-called "love" for her quickly turned to distaste.

Why does this happen? It happens because whether or not a man or woman chooses to embrace the Word of God, the same spiritual principles apply. They are built into the spirit of women and men to line up with the laws that God decreed from the beginning. No matter how liberal a couple is, once they sleep together a horrible little word crawls into the bed and snuggles up between them under the covers. That word is *obligation*. Both parties feel it. Most women give their bodies because they want to feel loved and connected. Once the act is completed, they expect the reward of commitment. After all, if you've given your whole being to this man, it seems only fair.

Years ago a very popular song said, "Tonight you're mine completely, you give your love so sweetly, so tell me now and I won't ask again, will you still love me tomorrow?" Those words are tinged with fear and desperation—and have set many a man on the run. When men wake up and find obligation staring them in the face, their spirits recoil. And women feel that recoil. This starts a chain reaction: We cling, they pull away, we cling harder and the cycle goes on and on and on.

Get the picture? I think we've all either been there or have seen this happen to our friends. The world calls this "making love." The truth is, if the love isn't already there, you certainly cannot create it.

Sex and Soul Ties

It is far more painful to break up with someone you've slept with than with someone you haven't. That's because God created sex to be the seal of marriage, to bind two people together. Sex is not just a pleasurable experience or an expression of love. It creates a soul tie whether love is present or not. The Word says "the two shall become one flesh."

When the relationship is severed, the soul is torn. This can be likened to peeling a potato or tearing the bark off a tree. Sounds agonizing, doesn't it? God never intended for us to endure that kind of pain. Yet it is a pain He can't allow us to escape because it's a consequence of sin. Yes, God will forgive us, but He cannot protect us from burning ourselves if we choose to touch the stove. He did His part—He warned us. We make the choice. His choice for us is men who will commit willingly out of a heartfelt decision, not because of overbearing obligation.

This soul tie was designed for our own security. When a man commits out of pure love, not tainted by lust and selfish motives, a woman knows she is desired as a person not an object. When this process is circumvented by premature sexual relations, it lays a foundation for distrust. The man is never sure you won't yield just as easily to another man. The woman starts to use sex as a weapon in the marriage because she feels that's how she got what she wanted in the first place.

But manipulation can be very dangerous. Even the Shulamite woman in Song of Songs knew it was not a good idea to "stir up nor awaken love until it pleases." She had been counseled by her brothers that if she were a wall, they would build towers of silver on her; but, if she were a door, they would enclose her with boards of cedar. In other words, if she kept herself pure, she would be honored, but if she allowed men to come into her (in the sexual sense), she would be punished by death according to the laws (cedar was used for burial coffins).

This young woman was able to proudly answer her brothers, "I am a wall, and my breasts like towers; then I became in his eyes [her fiancé] as one bringing contentment." She had complete understanding that her "vineyard was hers to give," but not ahead of the appointed time. She got her man, and his love for her was apparent to all who observed. He was attaining an untouched prize; he knew she could be trusted. He respected her because she was a well-kept woman.

A Well-Kept Woman

Speaking of well-kept women, how would you feel about Jesus sitting in your bedroom watching you engage in a sexual situation He has not ordained? Would you be comfortable with that? Even if you left Him "sitting" in the living room, He would know what you're doing. How would you feel knowing He would be watching as the man left in the morning? Would you be that brazen if Jesus were a man you could literally see sitting in your home?

Jesus wants better things for you.

I encourage you to have faith in God. Believe you are "fearfully and wonderfully made." Look and behave like a well-kept woman. The man that God has reserved for you will see and recognize your specialness because you are the piece of himself that he's been missing. You will complete the puzzle of his life. Since women sometimes seem to know these things before men do, it's up to us to give them time to find out—without compromising ourselves. Remember, the things you do now will affect your relationship for the rest of your life. Build a solid foundation from the beginning, one that God can bless and build on.

Okay, I hear someone objecting, "How do we know that we will be sexually compatible if we don't check it out?" If you've listened to God's direction, and this is the man He created you for, believe me, everything will be wonderful. True love has a way of making things that way. God is interested in your sex life; He wants you to enjoy one another. When He created you He worked out all those fine details in anticipation of the day the two of you would be together.

So, in the meantime, chill out or take a cold shower and wait on the Lord! Trust Him, and He will renew your strength. He doesn't ask us to do anything we're incapable of doing: "God is faithful, who will not allow you to be tempted beyond what you are able, but with the temptation will also make the way of escape, that you may be able to bear it" (1 Corinthians 10:13).

You can cooperate with Him by making yourself accountable to a friend that you can trust. This always helps. Do whatever it takes to help you remain in the right position to receive all that God has for you. You know better than anyone what your weak points are and where you're most vulnerable. Be honest with yourself, be honest in your prayers, and make realistic choices about what situations you and your date can be involved in without driving one another crazy.

Going halfway is not an option. A man falls in love with you based on how he feels when he's with you. You do not want frustration to be on his list. Remember, if you don't turn on the stove and stir the pot, the contents won't boil. "Why does the responsibility always fall on the woman?" you complain. It's unfortunate, but true. It is a reality we all have to accept and deal with. In some ways, it may be built into the spirit of a man to test us. If so, it's up to us to handle it.

Now, please, that doesn't mean you should turn into a holy prude. Learn how to handle all things with balance. If the man starts making moves toward you, you do not have to lay hands on him or start praying in the Spirit and casting out devils! Don't squash his romantic nature so thoroughly that he can't even imagine wanting to marry you. You do not want to end up with a man who's nursing a bruised ego. It's alright to make him feel desirable, you just have to keep things under control.

Keeping a Rein on Romance

How do you stay in control without ruining the romance? The next time he leans toward your ear and starts whispering sweet somethings, make a power play that can only work in your favor and give him something else to consider. Simply bat those Spirit-filled eyes at him, gently remove his hand from whatever inappropriate place on your body he may have placed it, and very sweetly say:

> *From the moment your eyes touch mine*
> *you awaken my desire for a time*
> *when I will be free to act*
> *upon all that I'm feeling*
> *but now is not that time . . .*
> *for I prefer to see you*
> *through eyes unclouded by*
> *the longings of my senses*
> *to discover all that you are*
> *free of the ties that can bind prematurely*
> *and so I choose to tread lightly*
> *to neither awaken nor stir*
> *the flames of desire*

and wait for a time
when love's fire will illuminate
and not destroy . . .
but now is not that time. . . .

From the moment your hand touches mine
I close my eyes and pray for strength
letting feelings wash over me
that I should ignore
my flesh clinging to them for a moment
then relinquishing its hold
as my spirit gently reassures my heart
that there will be a time
for languishing in love's rivers
but now is not that time. . . .

From the moment that your spirit
reaches for mine
and our silence
screams louder than any words
making impetuous promises of tomorrow
and lasting love
I dare to anticipate
a moment when perhaps
after all is said and done
we will be one
free to give to one another
without any inhibitions
unfettered by torn consciences
and unwise violations
perhaps there will come a time
past this moment
when I will pour out my love for you
and crown you with my caresses
a time when we will be sure
we were created
one for the other
totally and completely justified

and undefiled . . .
perhaps there will come a time
past this moment
but now is not that time. . . .

And on that note, send the man home!

4
Dealing with Dreams

Whew! Good for you! Now that you've gotten off to a good start with "Mr. Right," let's talk about your state of mind. Back to our movie already in progress. After your wonderful dinner date, your man takes you home. You've just said goodbye and closed the door. You twirl around the room and, if you're not too intoxicated by the evening's events, you tidy up before retiring to bed and calling up your closest girlfriend to tell her all about the most wonderful night you've ever had in your life.

Of course, since this is your pal—the one who has agreed to hold you accountable—she asks the fatal question, "Well, did you . . . ?" You can truthfully answer that even though you wanted to devour him piece by piece, you were strong to the bitter end. You graciously accept her congratulations. After planning your wedding and how many children you will have, you say goodnight and snuggle up for sweet dreams. There will be no counting sheep or meditating on Scripture tonight!

Sweet Dreams

The movie picture goes to soft focus as you enter a dream state. If you were courageous enough to chronicle your dream on paper for this man, it would go something like this.

I close my eyes
    and fall
        upon the pillow of your lips
            and my mind wanders
        as you whisper romantic visions
            for my ears to see
                my secret longings to hear . . .
                and my imagination runs wild
                sampling all the possibilities
        of you and me
        me and you
    doing all the things
that lovers do . . .
    and my heart
        races against the dawn
            not wanting to let go of the fantasy
                of being completely yours
                    here in my dreams
                    where it's safe
                    where every desire I ever had
                is coming true . . .
    I cling to you
        and we are
            covered in dew
locked and entwined in each other's breath . . .
        and I am totally caught up
            in larger-than-life visions of us
                that seem so real
            I am totally convinced
        it's going to be glorious
    being loved by you . . .

To all you super Christians who have never entertained these sorts of dreams or imaginations: Congratulations! You may feel free to advance to the next chapter. But for those of you who have cherished such fantasies or night visions, I suggest you stick with me. Even though I can empathize with having this kind of experience, I hope you'll hear me when I tell you how dangerous these dreams can be.

The Bible reminds us that "there is a time for everything, and a season for every activity under heaven" (Ecclesiastes 3:1 NIV). Paul wrote that all things are lawful, but all things are not expedient. There is nothing wrong with having sexual thoughts about the man you love, but they should be confined to marriage. Yes, these thoughts will come if you are human and have blood pumping through your veins. But single women can't afford to allow fantasies like this to run rampant.

"Okay," you say, "first you tell me I can't have sex, now you tell me I can't even think about it!" Wait a minute. Before you head for the kitchen to bury yourself in chocolate cake or cookies in total despair, hear me out. (See, I know all about folks who have decided that food is the only thing that's legal.) Remember, you still have a wedding dress to get into.

As We Think, So We Are

Remember in chapter 3 when we discussed Amnon, the one who raped Tamar? That rape started in Amnon's thought life. The Bible states that he fantasized about her to the point of illness! By the time he got near her, he was beyond rational thinking. And you know the end of the story: Death, sponsored by runaway imaginations.

Proverbs 23:7 says, "As he thinks in his heart, so is he." In less formal terms: "You can't stop a bird from flying over your head, but you can stop it from making a nest and laying eggs in it." Eventually, we will act out our thoughts.

Our fantasies, if uncontrolled, have a way of exalting themselves against the knowledge of God's will for our lives. They begin to scream louder than the still, small voice of the Holy Spirit. Our fantasies begin to take on lives of their own. They loudly argue and strive to justify their existence, all the while reassuring us that they are quite harmless. If we persist in entertaining them, we will be following through to the action all too soon—and much to our own horror. We'll be echoing that age-old phrase: "It just happened!"

Sorry, honey. Nothing "just happens." Fruit doesn't just grow. Something has to feed the roots in order to produce those succulent treats that we love to feast on. And all those hot, passionate imaginings are roots destined to produce the object of your thoughts—whether that's your intention or not. We make things hard on ourselves when we choose to dwell on our fantasies because they usually bring us to a fork in the road. Depending on how important our relationship with Christ is, we will either choose the path of compromise or the path of obedience. That choice is partially determined by how much time we've invested in our daydreams. In James 1:14,15 we read, "Each one is tempted when he is drawn away by his own desires and enticed. Then, when desire has conceived, it gives birth to sin; and sin, when it is full-grown, brings forth death."

Think of your daydreams and imaginations as subliminal advertising. Have you ever been watching television and all of a sudden you're starving—but you just ate? Then, as you finish whatever it is you've found to munch on, the thought occurs to you that it was that McDonald's commercial that got your appetite all revved up.

"Yeah, yeah, yeah, enough already," you say. "I got it! So what's a girl supposed to think about?"

Mind Over Imaginings

First of all, don't get upset. Understand that you are a healthy human being. Human beings are naturally inclined to have very active thought lives. Just be honest with yourself about what your thoughts have the potential to produce. God doesn't tell you not to have thoughts at all. What He does suggest, however, is that you think about things that are just and pure; about whatever is lovely or of good report. He wants you to think on things that have virtue or are praiseworthy. This will require some work on your part.

You are going to have to cast down those imaginations that exalt themselves against the knowledge of what you know to be God's will. You have to consciously work on corralling your thoughts, holding them captive, and lining them up in obedience to Christ.

Taking Out the Garbage

Is your thought life obedient to Christ? Or are you treating it like a junk closet or a makeshift storage area? Is it so crammed with odds and ends that you no longer know what's in there? Be honest with yourself, but don't despair. Since God gave the command to purify your thought life, He is going to give you whatever amount of grace you need to be obedient to Him. But you've got to be willing to call your thought life what it is. If it's junky, fling open that closet and show it to Jesus! He's waiting to help you clean it up. He doesn't mind. He's a wonderful roommate because He believes in sharing chores—especially the kind that involves cleaning.

However, cleaning up our thought life is definitely swimming upstream. The world encourages us to go with the flow, to follow our feelings and natural inclinations. There's only one small problem. Our natural inclinations are in rebellion against God. And our hearts and minds can be deceitful. Most of the time we aren't even aware of what we're harboring. There are certain things we just don't want to deal with. We figure they aren't in the way of anything significant, so they couldn't possibly cause any trouble.

Have you ever left something in the refrigerator too long? Finally, one day you open it and "Ugh!" Something bears a striking resemblance to something you saw on television crawling across the screen devouring people and whole cities! Our minds can become like that. So much for going with the flow—you'll either drown or be consumed. Get rid of the garbage! And don't forget that Jesus has His sleeves rolled up, and He's ready and roaring to go. "If we confess our sins, [Jesus] is faithful and just to forgive us our sins and to cleanse us from all unrighteousness" (1 John 1:9). So come on, repent and 'fess up. You'll be so proud of yourself when you're finished. It's God's will for you to be able to live with yourself and, besides, He'd like to have a little more room to make Himself at home in your thought life.

The Turning Point

Where shall we begin? First, pinpoint the things that get your imaginations careening down the road of self-indulgence. It's important to note that this exercise is a highly individual thing. Some people can watch a good love story and not trip, some people can't. So what about that movie that had smoke coming out of your ears the other night? Be honest with yourself about what you can handle. If mood music really does put you "in the mood," you should avoid it until you can really put it to use. You need to do your own spot check and make the conscious decision not to entertain anything that fuels the revolt of your senses against the will of God. Choose to guard your heart and your mind. Keep your eye on the prize—a God-ordained marriage. You want to arrive at your destination in one piece, untarnished.

Renewing Our Minds

We know thoughts can work for us or against us. Let's make our thought life work for us. Let's make it propel us toward a healthy relationship. How? Begin by flushing out the old and bringing in the new. Fill your mind with the Word of God. Reflect on who and whose you are. Decide that you want to mirror God's Word. Remember, you have a reputation to protect. You are God's well-kept woman. You are a virtuous woman whose price is far above rubies. You and your body are a valuable commodity.

As you renew your mind, you will not be conformed to the world. Satan will not be able to approach you with his rationalizations on how you should let little fantasies slide. You will begin to measure your thoughts against the Word of God and dispose of anything that doesn't measure up to His criteria of being acceptable. Remember, whatever is in you will come out.

As you fill your mind with godly thoughts and imaginations, something wonderful will take place inside of you. You will have more power to deal with temptation when it presents itself because the Word of God will automatically rise up to meet it. You will be free of tension. You won't spend every moment with the man of your dreams torn between lust and the dread of carrying out what you're feeling. This opens the door to really have quality time with your Mr. Right, to really and truly become friends and to learn how to enjoy one another outside of the bedroom (which, by the way, is where you will spend most of your free time—even if you're married).

What a refreshing thought! On a more subtle level, you will be building trust between yourselves for the future, not to mention a whole lot of respect. So let's hear it for swimming upstream! It's hard work, but worth every minute, and there is a reward at the end of the river.

Dreaming—God's Way

Now, since God never takes something away without replacing it, I'd like to replace that first daydream. I believe it should go something like this:

On our wedding night
when we consummate our love
when our spirits kiss
and the angels sing in harmony
with our melody . . .
when your breath fills my world
with the sweet perfume of your inner being . . .
when God sits at the foot of our bed
and applauds our union . . .
when our souls fuse together

> in an eternal embrace our flesh
>> will never know . . .
> then the universe will acknowledge
>> as we agree
>>> that "it is good" . . .
> until then
>> I will patiently store my love for you
>>> in an inner well
>>>> and wait for the day
>>>>> when I can drench you in it
>>>>>> again . . .
>>>>>> and again . . .
>>>>> on our wedding night . . .
>>>> and the stars will smile
>>> and the wind will laugh
>>> and the moon
>>>> will stand as a silent witness . . .
>>> then the heavens will ring out
>>>> as we agree
>>>>> that "it is good" . . .

Now that is a daydream you can quietly tuck away in your heart and mind without condemnation or fear.

Sorting Out Old Baggage

There is one last area of thought life that deserves a comment or two: old baggage from past relationships. Again, Jesus will help you with this. Ask Him to guide you as you sort out which lessons should be kept for personal reference and which old rags should be thrown away and forgotten. Whatever you do, don't superimpose any negative past experiences on your new relationship. You don't want to find yourself battling monsters that don't exist.

Start with a clean slate and await God's instruction. Continue to maintain your well-kept position, which is one of confidence. Trust God to deliver His promise to you—He will give you the desires of your heart.

5
Promises, Promises

Once upon a time there was a Christian woman who met a wonderful man. He wasn't a Christian, but he was interested in hearing what she had to say about her relationship with God. As their friendship progressed, he said and did all the right things, and this young woman's heart was stirred. Not only was he fun to be with and a fulfillment of all her fantasies, he respected the fact that she didn't want to compromise her Christian standards by sleeping with him. He even stated he was ready for marriage and marveled at how any man could ever have allowed her to escape his grasp. After all, she was so extraordinary any man in his right mind would want to spend the rest of his life with her.

How fortunate could a woman get? In response, she politely took her heart out of the protective hand of Jesus and gave it to this wonderful man. She did so, fully believing that God would honor her chastity and miraculously save him. They would ride off into the sunset as man and wife and live happily ever after.

Well, this is where the plot takes a very sad turn. Although this man admired the woman's commitment to God, he felt no accountability to God himself. He had no concept of why he should not yield to his sexual desires. In fact, in his world the notion of denying the flesh was totally alien. He decided that all this holiness was beginning to wear on his manhood, so he presented the idea that the two of them should be "just friends." He then began seeing someone else who was more willing to comply to his wishes and what he termed "his needs."

Oh, but the story doesn't end there! The man's new love interest became pregnant. The man, being upright and moral, though of the worldly persuasion, married the young woman. This left the Christian lady totally devastated. She had believed that he would get over this "friendship" thing, come to his senses, get saved, and marry her if she just allowed him to get the silly notion that you have to sleep with someone to be in love with her out of his head. With her hopes and dreams of a perfect future laying in shambles around her feet, the devil invited himself to tea, armed with deadly questions and croissants laced with self-pity.

The young Christian woman was me.

How to Have a Pity Party

Getting emotionally involved with an unsaved man was my first mistake. The second mistake—and an even more dangerous one—was having tea with the devil. He was more than happy to brew up his own special blend of unbelief tea and heap a great big slice of resignation pie topped with why-me sauce onto my plate. Sound familiar? We all have a story to tell about how we began to question God's provision for our heartfelt desires.

"That's what you get for being so holy," my hateful tea companion gleefully scolded. "You don't really believe that any man—saved or unsaved—is ever going to marry you without sleeping with you first, do you?" To my horror, I felt myself sinking into reluctant agreement.

He continued. "Furthermore, it's time to cut out this waiting-on-God stuff. You have to go after what you want and make it happen. God doesn't care if you ever get married. As a matter of fact, He would prefer that you remain single so that He can have all your attention. He's selfish that way. You keep up this 'super Christian' bit and you'll be old and gray before you crawl down the aisle. All your best years will be behind you, and you'll have no energy left to have the kind of honeymoon night that would make up for all your waiting."

The devil wasn't finished with his little monologue. "And what about all those kids you wanted to have? You're not Sarah, you know. Your body isn't going to always look great, and you're going to end up with some man that looks even worse. Now that's a fine reward for holiness."

On and on he went, serving up his tidbits of gloom and doom. Well, after that first sip of unbelief tea, anything he sat in front of me looked worth sampling, so I eagerly scooped up each morsel until I became quite ill. Once he had me lying in a heap of despair on my bed, my evil visitor viewed his handiwork with satisfaction, decided that his mission had been accomplished, and abandoned me in pursuit of another victim.

The Truth About Kisses

Now an even worse fate awaited me. I was left alone with my own thoughts. But while I was content to continue my mental pity party, Jesus and the Holy Spirit held a quiet conference in the corner of my room. The voices of my thoughts grew louder and louder, expressing every fear, disappointment, and grievance about the way God was running my life. Actually, I can't remember which was louder—my tears, my thoughts, or the sound of me blowing my nose. Somewhere in the midst of all the hubbub, I finally muttered, "Help me, Jesus," and fell into a fitful sleep.

Upon awakening, I was greeted by the Holy Spirit who very gently said, "Do you feel better now?"

Recalling the pain, I eked out a froggy sounding "No . . . "

"Are you at least ready to listen to our side of the story, or would you rather dwell on the comments of your former tea-party guest?" The Lord was still speaking in His gracious voice.

"Okay," I sighed, "I'm ready to listen."

"First of all," He said, taking a deep breath, "your tea partner is a liar. There is only One who tells you the truth, whose promises are yea and amen. He is not a man that He should lie, nor just the Son of man that He should change His mind. He acts upon what He has spoken and fulfills every promise He makes. The choice is yours, Who will you choose to trust? My child, don't you know . . .

> *Kisses aren't promises*
> > *they carry no warranties*
> > > *guaranteeing a lifetime of service*
> > > *or love*
> > *they are but the hunger of two hearts*
> > *for the moment*
> > *the longing to touch*
> > > *beneath the surface*
> > > > *to sample the very essence*
> > > > *of one's soul*
> *to taste*
> > *to explore*
> > > *to experience one's breath*
> > > *and perhaps*
> > > > *draw life from it . . .*
> > > > *gently probing*
> > > *pressing past outward appearances*
> > > *and reservations*
> > > > *connecting . . .*
> > > > > *prying . . .*
> > > > *nudging each other's*
> > > > *consciences and desires*
> > > > > *into awakening*
> > > *challenging one another's inhibitions*
> > > *in a gentle game*
> > > > *of truth or dare*
> > *kissing . . .*
> > > *touching . . .*
> > > > *leaving a portion*

of one's inner self behind
sometimes meaning to return to the well
for yet another drink
sometimes not
for the cord
has been broken
only the sweet aroma
of two spirits once intertwined
remains to dissipate
into unspoken memories
and feelings never vocalized . . .
no promises made . . .
no promises kept . . .
after all
kisses never have been
and never will be
promises . . .

I have to admit, my afternoon tea session with the devil had left me with a slight case of amnesia concerning God's promises. So back to the Word I went to refresh my memory. First, I took a look at some case histories. Then I considered God's comments on marriage, on love, and on what His intentions were for my life. Hopefully, what I rediscovered will help dispel some myths you may have chosen to harbor in the midst of your own disappointments.

Marriage: God's Invention

Let's consider God's first comment about relationships: "It is not good that man should be alone" (Genesis 2:18). After He came to that conclusion, He created the woman for the man. I think it's safe to say that God doesn't think it's good for woman to be alone, either . . . unless you possess "the gift," and you probably wouldn't be reading this book if you had it.

When it comes to marriage, God is deeply involved. I think it is essential to remember that the heart of kings is in God's hands. He is the great orchestrator of all things. He is able to keep people apart or bring them together. He is able to harden a heart or soften it. It is the Holy Spirit that draws God's children toward one another when He wants to, whether His ultimate purpose is marriage or not.

But don't go getting mad at God for every failed relationship you've ever had. If He allowed it to fail, He was saving you from something you would not have been able to endure. Have you ever looked back at an old boyfriend and wondered what on earth you ever saw in him? Did you hoot in dismay over the fact that you were once desperately in love with him and thought that life without him was out of the question? How little we see when we're close-up; how revealing a step back can be. Don't ever lose sight of one of the most profound promises of God—"All things work together for good to those who love God, to those who are called according to His purpose" (Romans 8:28). That means you!

Isaac and Rebekah

When Abraham decided it was time for his son Isaac to get married, he gave his most trusted servant instructions to return to Abraham's homeland and select a bride for his son. (He didn't want Isaac getting involved with the foreign women of the region where they were living.) The servant obediently set out to accomplish his master's wishes. When he reached the place where Abraham's relatives lived, he prayed and asked God to reveal to him the woman who was right for Isaac by moving her to exhibit a spirit that was willing to serve.

About that time, a young woman named Rebekah came to the well to draw water. When the servant asked her for a drink of water, she cheerfully responded by offering to water his camels as well. The servant concluded that she was the one.

The Bible takes special pains to point out that Rebekah was beautiful and a virgin. I believe when God dictated the Word, He didn't waste any words—every word that was written bears deep significance. Rebekah's virginity was important to God.

As the perfect order of God would have it, Rebekah was a member of Abraham's family clan, and she was willing to follow the servant back to the land where Abraham and Isaac were living. Both of these conditions had been specific requirements given by Abraham. The summation of these events was love at first sight between Isaac and Rebekah. They were married, and along came a set of twins, the youngest part of the direct blood-line of Jesus Christ.

To me, this story in Genesis can be an analogy for one of God's promises of relationship. Look at it this way: Abraham typifies your heavenly Father. And God knows exactly where your husband is and where you are. At the time He deems appropriate, He will send the Holy Spirit (represented by the servant) to design your meeting and coming together. There are two requirements in God's mind of what will make a blessed union.

First and foremost, both people must belong to the family of God. The Bible says we are not to be unequally yoked together with unbelievers. Although human beings are all God's creation, not all are claimed as His children. We have to acknowledge Him as Father and yield to His authority before we can walk in the confidence that we have been adopted out of the world and into His family. Only through repentance and confession of His Lordship are we translated from illegitimacy into a family that is a royal priesthood.

Being equally yoked requires more than two people being Christians. It helps when people have the same backgrounds and share complementary goals and values. Two becoming one is a lot easier to achieve when both parties are walking in the same direction, which brings me to the second point of this story: Rebekah had to be willing to go to where Isaac was.

As women of God, we have to be willing to be a support system to our husbands, no matter where they are in life. I'm not talking about just physical location, either. I am referring to where they are emotionally, mentally, and spiritually. We cannot go into a relationship and marriage planning to change or move a man from where he is. That is God's job and depends on what He decides needs to be changed. We'll deal with that in more detail later.

Jacob and Rachel

Let's look at Jacob and Rachel. Their story drums up images of a lost art in today's society—the art of courtship leading to marriage without premarital sex. Jacob loved Rachel so much that he agreed to work for her father for *seven* years in order to have Rachel as his wife. The Bible says that the seven years were like only a few days to Jacob because he loved her so much.

Mind you, Jacob had to complete the seven years work before he could marry Rachel and sleep with her, dispelling the myth about men not marrying women they haven't slept with. Yes, there can be marriage before sex—even today.

Much to Jacob's dismay, upon completion of his seven year's work Rachel's father gave him her sister Leah instead. He then conned Jacob into working another seven years in order to have Rachel. In spite of the fact that Rachel had not allowed Jacob to sample her "wares," he agreed to work another seven years for her hand. How's that for pure, strong, true love?

Ruth and Boaz

One more story before I reveal the next promise. It's time to revisit Ruth—you know, the one with perfect timing and the capacity to recognize and take good advice? (See chapter 1.) Ruth went to glean for grain in the field of Boaz, who, besides being a kind and wealthy man, was also a kinsman of her deceased husband. Ruth was acting under the advisement of her mother-in-law, Naomi. Well, as God would have it, Boaz noticed Ruth and decided to make special provision for her. He also admonished his hired help not to bother her in any way. He went out of his way to welcome her and make her feel at home.

Boaz ordered his servants that even if Ruth made a mistake and gleaned from where she wasn't supposed to, they were not to embarrass her. He went on to give them instructions to leave extra sheaves for her to find, and he told her to remain in his fields, close to his workers, where she would be safe. After some time had progressed, per Naomi's direction, Ruth washed and perfumed herself and went down to the threshing floor where Boaz was sleeping. She laid down at his feet and covered herself with the edge of his garment. When he awoke with a start and inquired why she was there, she presented her need to him.

Jewish law stated that when a woman's husband died, the next of kin was to marry her in order to carry on the family name. Boaz was flattered that she would come to him instead of a younger man. But there was one slight problem: There was a closer kinsman who had the right to marry her. If this kinsman did not want to claim her, Boaz would. He told Ruth to stay where she was until morning and to be careful not to let anyone see her leaving the threshing floor. In the morning, before she left, he made sure to load her up with provisions to take home.

When she returned to Naomi, Ruth relayed everything that had taken place. Naomi wisely commented, "Wait my daughter, until you find out what happens. For the man will not rest until the matter is settled today."

Don't tell me older women don't know what they're talking about! They have seen it all. Sure enough, Boaz immediately went out to take care of business. Not only was he a good man, he was a shrewd man and a master negotiator. He went to his kinsman and propositioned him about buying the land that belonged to Ruth's dead husband, yielding to his first right to purchase it since he was the next kinsman in line. Of course the kinsman-redeemer was interested in purchasing the land.

That's when Boaz added the condition that in order for him to purchase the land, he also had to take Ruth as part of the package according to the law. Based on that revelation, the kinsman was not willing to pay the price, so he conceded his right to the land and Ruth to Boaz. As a result, Boaz and Ruth were married and became the proud great-great grandparents of David the king.

There's a popular old song that says, "When a man loves a woman, can't keep his mind on nothin' else, he'll tell the world about the good thing he's found." The simple truth of that song is intertwined in the second promise from God concerning your mate. In both of the stories I've shared, the men were willing to pay the price in order to win their brides. They were compelled to protect and nurture their women.

Paying the Price

Another promise of God, as you've probably guessed by now, is that when He places you in front of the man He has chosen for you, that man will be willing to pay the price. He will be willing to give up all he considers valuable, including sex, in order to have you. As a matter of fact, he won't want anything to be out of order. He won't put you in any situation where your reputation stands the chance of being marred. He will be protective of everything concerning you, including your walk with the Lord. He will love you enough not to lead you into compromise. He will willingly take his place as leader, protector, and provider.

If he doesn't, look out!

Boaz was very careful to protect Ruth's reputation and make sure she did not suffer the lack of anything she needed. Her comfort and satisfaction were of the utmost importance to him.

Joseph and Mary

On to the next promise and one last story. When Mary was told by the angel that she had been chosen to bear the Messiah, the Son of God, it was a privilege she humbly accepted. But it presented a problem—she was engaged to Joseph. According to the law, if a woman was betrothed or engaged to a man and she slept with someone else, she could be stoned to death for adultery. Since Mary was pregnant, it would be natural for anyone to assume that she had been busy—and it hadn't been with Joseph!

Mary went to Joseph and told him everything that had happened, and all the angel had told her. I think one of two things happened at that time in Joseph's mind: 1) He had a hard time believing her, but he couldn't be sure. Something kept him from reaching a final verdict on the matter; 2) He really believed her, but couldn't really see how he fit into the picture.

Either way, in order to spare her, Joseph decided to put her away privately so that she would not be stoned (there's that protectiveness again). But the angel of the Lord wasn't finished delivering messages. He appeared to Joseph and confirmed what Mary had told him. He then urged Joseph not to be afraid to take Mary as his wife, that this was indeed the hand of God in order to fulfill God's promise of a Messiah to His people. So Joseph took Mary to be his wife and had no sexual relations with her until she gave birth to Jesus. How's that for maintaining self-control and being willing to wait for the woman you love?

He Can't Get Away!

Another promise is that you can't miss what God has for you. "Your" man cannot get away! The Holy Spirit will be on his case big time until he lines up with God's chosen plan for his life. You must remember that God ordains every detail of our lives in order to place us in the most effective position for the kingdom of God. Marriage is one of those positions. When God decides you will be more effective for Him in marriage, He speaks it, and it is so. It's important for us to have a bigger picture of marriage beyond our personal desires. Marriage isn't just about reaching a much-wanted destination. It goes further than that. In God's plan it reaches beyond us to the surrounding community and, perhaps, even to the world.

Marriage is designed to be an integral part of kingdom business. It is a ministry, therefore God is profoundly interested in our marriage plans. He wants them to line up with His plans. Joseph and Mary were called to raise the Son of God. To what might He be calling you and your husband? To raise a child who might one day be a great minister? To have a ministry of your own? To develop a marriage that sets a good example and glorifies God's name to people around you? Great or small, it's all ministry, and it's all important to God. This is crucial to understand so you can carry out the ministry of marriage effectively. When God decides that's where you will be most effective, you won't be able to miss it!

The Word says that the blessings of the Lord will overtake us. That's good news that sets us free! That means that no matter what mistakes we make, we cannot usurp the calendar of events that God has planned. One last story backs up that statement.

Sarah was married to Abraham, a man who truly believed the promises of God. But there was one promise Sarah couldn't believe: that she would bear a child and be the mother of many nations. Well, at the age of 90 it was no small wonder that she had trouble believing! But God meant what He said, and said what He meant. Despite the fact that Sarah chose to take matters into her own hands, God carried out His plan. Sarah's plan was to have her handmaid bear Abraham's child. When her handmaid gave birth to a child, nothing turned out as Sarah had planned. Even though her plan failed, it did not circumvent God's declaration that she was to be the grand mama of a mighty nation.

At the appointed time, God chose to glorify Himself by fulfilling His promise, and He did so in the face of seemingly impossible circumstances. Sarah bore Abraham a child in her old age. Yes, God delights in impossible situations; they are opportunities to prove His power, His love, and His determination to fashion us into overcomers. So who are you going to trust in the light of such wonderful promises?

Rehearsing the Promises

Learn how to silence the enemy by rehearsing God's promises over and over again until they are embedded deeply in your spirit. God has promised to perfect all things concerning you. He is not in the business of serving up half-baked cookies. You don't want to partake in that kind of fare, anyway. Trust His timing for your life because He is busy fulfilling His purpose for you.

In the meantime, allow God to hold on to your heart. He is able to keep what we commit to Him; it's like placing it in a safe. He's not going to turn it over to just anyone. He knows who will take good care of it and who will be willing to pay the price for it. Admit to yourself that you haven't done a good job of keeping your heart safe from abuse and hand it over to Him.

I failed to mention that even though God still had His way and fulfilled the promise of Sarah having a child, she was forced to deal with the consequences of her own handiwork. Hagar, her handmaid, bore Abraham a son, and the boy was named Ishmael. This was not the child that Abraham had been promised—that child was to come from the womb of Sarah.

You see, Sarah didn't get it. God had His program already in process, with the universe as an audience. Nothing was going to stop His performance, whether the actors chose to believe in opening night or not. So up went the curtain and Sarah had a son, Isaac. The heavens applauded. But there was a loose string in the orchestra creating discord—Hagar's son, Ishmael.

These two brothers created a rift that is still at war today, acted out in the roles of Israel and the Arab nations. If only Sarah had waited! The consequences of not allowing God to deliver His promise according to His plans and His time schedule affected more than just Sarah and Abraham. Their impatience and lack of trust affected the entire world. In similar terms, the choices you make rebound far beyond your personal space. They affect more people than you will ever know.

As a reward for the wait, your heavenly Father promises that "no eye has seen, no ear has heard, no mind has conceived what God has prepared for those who love him" (1 Corinthians 2:9 NIV). Why? Because He is able and anxious to do abundantly, above all that you can ask or think (see Ephesians 3:20).

When God presents you to your mate, it is going to be better than you ever imagined because God does all things well. Furthermore, He doesn't intend to sell any of us cheap. We are a valuable commodity, and He is committed to preserving and maintaining our upkeep. He gave His Word that "the desire of the righteous will be granted" (Proverbs 10:24). That's a promise every well-kept woman of God can take to heart. It's His promise, and God *always* keeps His promises.

6
The Awakening

Now that we've established some very important foundations, we're ready to move on to the ins-and-outs of relationships. No matter how in love you are, there is no such thing as a perfect, trouble-free partnership. That's why it's important to be clear about who you are and what God has promised regarding your life.

It's been said that the greatest fear is the fear of the unknown. When we know what is getting ready to happen, we can usually prepare ourselves and map out a scenario as to how we would like things to go. When we don't, unexpected events intrude on our perfect plan, and even the most composed Spirit-filled woman can go off on a tangent. We can plan responses, but reactions usually have a life all their own.

With that in mind, I would like to prepare you for one "surprise" that tends to happen in new relationships.

A Man's Divided Self

Let's tune back in to our ongoing movie. We'll pick up at the scene where you have decided that yes, all the pieces fit. This has to be the most wonderful man you've ever encountered: you have so much in common, you're comfortable together, you and he are good friends, plus the chemistry is right. You're pretty sure you've received the all-clear signal in your spirit this is "the one," and that you're the missing rib from this man's side. So there you sit, the glow of love radiating from your face, basking in the wonderment of your newfound relationship.

He, on the other hand, is having a completely different set of thoughts, and it's not about what color wallpaper should go in the master bedroom. Panic is setting in, and his anxieties are quickly rising to the surface in the form of some very real fears and questions. So while you sit peacefully watching a late night movie together after a perfectly wonderful evening out (it usually happens after a perfect date that makes you even more optimistic than usual), his mind starts churning out thoughts like this:

> *You run your fingers through my hair*
> *grip my spirit*
> *and crawl inside my soul . . .*
> *causing me to reflect*
> *on how very much*
> *a part of me you've become*
> *in such a short space of time . . .*
> *and as you ramble through the chasms*
> *of my inner self*
> *awakening sleeping emotions*
> *disturbing private resolutions*
> *tickling touchy subjects*
> *confronting silent fears . . .*
> *I feel a strange mixture of emotions . . .*
> *my heart swells to accommodate*
> *what my divided self*
> *angrily chooses to view*
> *as an unwelcome intrusion*
> *of my intimate space . . .*
> *and I am torn . . .*
> *for I realize*

that receiving you
means yielding to you . . .
being naked to you . . .
being vulnerable to your rejection
of all that I am . . .
or maybe just a small portion
but large to me just the same . . .
and if by chance
you accept me
with all my "isms"
there looms an even larger question . . .
am I really willing to divorce myself
to become totally one with you . . .
or will I continue
to allow my selfishness
to let fear mediate with my reasoning
that it is
far better
to flirt
with the fires of love
than to be consumed
by the heat of it . . .

On that note, he tenderly kisses you goodnight, says he'll talk to you tomorrow, then disappears for a couple of days. When he resurfaces, he mumbles something evasive about having to take care of some business; or depending on where the needle on his fear monitor is, he says he's been thinking that he needs some "space," or he has decided that the two of you should "just be friends"!

Does this sound familiar? Let me interject that *if* this situation should arise, the duration of this behavior will be based on how long it takes God to accomplish what He is trying to work out in both of you. Also, at least in part, your reaction to the man's actions influence the outcome.

Choosing the Right Response

Now, before you quickly misplace God's relationship promises, and before you react to the man in a tone of voice that would make one stop to wonder if it was live or Memorex, push the pause button and calmly select a response that could work in your favor.

Are you ready for this? It's really rather simple. What you do is take a deep breath and quietly say, "Well, if you really think that's best, okay."

Next, if you don't already have one, I suggest you get a life. This accomplishes two things. First, you won't sit around wasting your time in quiet desperation, pining for the phone to ring or his car to drive up. Second, it gives him something to think about if you're not so readily available. Otherwise, he may be tempted to string you along for awhile. Many a man will check to see if you're saving his space while he's taking his relationship sabbatical.

As a wise, male friend of mine once said, "A man will spend a lifetime chasing what he cannot have." In short, every man needs to know beyond a shadow of a doubt that he misses your presence. You must give him the opportunity to find that out. (Make sure you don't get carried away and turn this into a game. Remember, he is a child of God, too.)

Before you go through a series of hysterical gyrations and blood-curdling protests, let's consider a few points. First of all, if this is the man God has selected for you, the issue of commitment goes beyond your limited vision. We are now dealing with a larger concern—that of submitting to the will of God. This is usually preceded by a fight that takes place on two levels, first spiritual, then natural.

The natural part of the fight is what I call the "clanging gate" syndrome. When a man feels the tug on his heart to make a commitment, no matter how wonderful a time he is having with you the word "forever" sounds like an iron gate cutting off his access to Freedom Highway.

If You Love Him, Set Him Free

Freedom is of the utmost importance to a man. A woman longs to be possessed; a man longs to be free. Don't be insulted by that. The enemy has told the man that to love you and commit to you is bondage. A man needs to know he can have you and his freedom, too, and he will put you to the test to ensure his peace of mind. See it for what it is, and don't over-react.

The truth is, freedom is an essential ingredient to any relationship, including our relationship with God. He created us as free agents. He doesn't coerce us into loving Him. He doesn't manipulate us into dependency on Him. He allows His consistency of love to draw us into choosing to be faithful to Him. Take a lesson from God, who is love.

"That's easier said than done," you say. "My future is on the line. I've got a life to catch. . . ." Well, there's an adage that might sound trite at this stage of the game, but that doesn't cancel out the validity of its message: "If you love someone, set him free." If people are meant to be in our lives, they will return of their own volition.

This stage of the relationship is what separates the girls from the women. It examines our powers of restraint, exaggerates our greatest fears, and exposes our perception of our self-worth. Most of all, it tests our faith. At a time like this, it is crucial to review God's promises. Remember, *if it is God's will, it will happen!* If it is not God's will, it's better for you to find out early in the game so you can be free to receive the person God has chosen for you.

In case you are still a little shaky about letting go of your dream man (lest he disappear over the horizon line never to be seen or heard from again), let me give you a few examples of the apprehending power of God. Keep in mind that free will is still very much involved. It's important to understand that God is not going to make this man fall in love with you. God will simply allow the circumstances of this man's life to reveal what is already in his heart.

Time Out in the Whale's Belly

Let's take a look at a guy by the name of Jonah. According to the book of Jonah, God commanded him to go and prophesy to the city of Ninevah. Instead, Jonah chose to disobey God and go in the opposite direction. He boarded a ship which got caught in a violent storm. The storm was brought on by Jonah's disobedience, and it resulted in his getting thrown overboard. Then he was swallowed by a great fish!

Jonah had a lot of time to think and weigh his options inside the belly of the cruise-liner God had prepared for him. After three days and three nights, Jonah cried out to God. I'm sure he had to process anger and a whole set of other emotions before he clearly came to the conclusion that God's way is best. And seeing that he was unable to control his own circumstances probably helped him reach the verdict that it would be to his advantage to follow God's orders. My favorite part of Jonah's prayer is this:

> When my life was ebbing away, I remembered you, LORD, and my prayer rose to you, to your holy temple. Those who cling to worthless idols forfeit the grace that could be theirs. But I, with a song of thanksgiving, will sacrifice to you. What I have vowed I will make good. Salvation comes from the LORD (Jonah 2:7-9 NIV).

Jonah had received an order from God. He made a decision that directly opposed the order, and he ran from the presence of the Lord. From that moment, his life went downhill: *Down* to Tarshish, *down* into the ship, *down* into the sea, *down* into the belly of the great fish. *Down, down, down.* In fact, he almost took an entire crew of sailors with him! God is not obligated to protect us when we remove ourselves from under the umbrella of obedience to Him.

So Jonah sat in the belly of the fish. He probably stewed and fretted and rationalized how what he did was justifiable. He bemoaned his circumstances and questioned the love of God. And God waited. God waited until Jonah recognized His sovereignty and yielded to it. It was the yielding that released Jonah. God spoke to the fish, and the fish vomited Jonah onto dry land. God then repeated His original command. This time Jonah ran to do His bidding.

How does this story apply to your situation? If God has spoken to the man in your life and told him that you are the mate selected for him, and he chooses to run anyway, open the door and let him go. He will be back. Once he hits that door, the fish of life will swallow him up; the circumstances of his rebellion will swallow him up.

Those circumstances can present themselves in many forms: loneliness, dissatisfaction, lack of peace, another painful relationship. Whatever form it takes, when he emerges from it, the original command will stand, and by then he will be able to appreciate you for the blessing that you are.

Socializing with Swine

There's another biblical example of males in flight, this one involving the prodigal son. Remember him from Luke 15:11-32? Here was a man who didn't know when he had it made. He was living the good life, his world was filled with all the creature comforts anyone would want. He had a family that loved him, wealth, good food, a wonderful home, willing servants, and any other provision he could dream up. Yet this man was plagued by the nagging question, What else is out there? So he went to his father, asked for his share of the wealth, and went off to see the wizard. He never made it to the Emerald City.

The prodigal's expedition ended in poverty and shame. He found himself in a pig sty (which is ironic since he was used to living in a mansion). There he was hoping to beat the pigs, considered the lowest of the lowly beasts—unclean and untouchable—to the slop that was thrown their way to eat. Fortunately, he came to his senses and chose to honestly review his situation.

Upon realizing that the servants at his father's house ate better than he did, he decided to humble himself and go home. When his father saw him coming up the road, he went out to greet him with open arms, welcoming him back as if he had simply been away on a long vacation. What an example of compassion and forgiveness!

It isn't too hard to see the similarities between this story and certain modern-day relationships. Here you are in the middle of what you consider a wonderful relationship. You are being the epitome of perfection. You look good, smell good, do all the things that every man wants his woman to do. You embody the very essence of the woman of his fantasies. But in spite of all this, this misguided man gets the idea that there is something else out there—something more perfect than you! So off he goes to mingle with the swine.

Practicing Unconditional Love

Why not use the time he's away constructively? Instead of sitting around having powwows with your girlfriends, trying to figure out which strategy would be more effective for retrieving this man, get your heart in order. If you are human, two emotions will automatically emerge when this mini-crisis hits: hurt and indignation. Meanwhile, pride lurks somewhere in the background, putting its hand on its hip and loudly proclaiming, "You don't have to take this! When he returns, guess who won't be waiting!" Thank God that He doesn't harbor the same attitude when it comes to us.

Don't lose your faith, hope, and love simply because temporary insanity threatens your wedding date. Take, for instance, counterfeit money. It is commonly known that special agents are trained to recognize counterfeit bills by closely and thoroughly examining real dollars bills. After long and deliberate scrutinizing, they are able to quickly discern the fakes. You need to remember that when Boyfriend was with you, he encountered the real thing. Now he has no choice but to see any substitution as a sad imitation.

Also note that God allowed this situation to bring about changes in *both* of you. God doesn't waste anyone's time. This particular circumstance has an uncanny way of revealing what is really inside of you, and knowledge is a very necessary component of character building. Imagine that we are gold nuggets. In order for us to be fashioned into valuable and functional vessels worthy of use or exhibition, we have to be purified and shaped. This calls for heat. Nothing can be more painful than meltdown, but it's the only way to remove the impurities.

Maybe you've never realized how much unforgiveness you can harbor. Or how much anger is affecting what words you let come out of your mouth. These are just two of the issues God likes to improve in us to get us ready for a long-term commitment. These attitudes can be very damaging to a relationship and cause needless pain and division.

It is extremely important not to start leveling the blame at your partner gone AWOL. Instead, turn to God and ask Him what He wants to work out in *you*. You might consider keeping a journal of your feelings and the things God reveals to you during this time. You will be amazed at what you'll learn about yourself and how your perspective will change if you submit your heart to the Lord and allow Him to complete what He started in you. When He brings the two of you back together, you will be able to exchange notes and share insights.

The Right Man at the Right Time

When my own situation went awry, I found that I was a very angry person. I harbored "rights" that were not mine to hold onto. I was horrified to see how covetous I was, how prone I was to criticize when I was hurt by the man I was dating. I questioned God and shook my puny little fist in His face. I told Him He had to take better control of my situation since, I felt, He had made me a promise and broken it. How could I trust Him any longer if He was going to extend lollipops and then be cruel enough to take them back?

After wrestling alone in the dark for several months, continually battling seething anger and frustration from not being able to diffuse my pain, I finally surrendered to God. I was forced to second Job's motion that "Though He slay me, yet will I trust Him" (Job 13:15).

When I reached that point, I was finally able to hear the Lord. He spoke to my spirit and soothed me. I was able to take all the hurt, anger, and shattered pieces of my heart and place them on the altar before Him. He picked up the fragments of that offering and began to replace them with His vision of the situation. He had not betrayed me. He did have a mate for me. Who was I to say that the end of the situation had been decreed?

A friend once told me, "One person's goodbye leaves the door open for the person God has truly chosen to say hello." Only when we are completely free are we in the position to respond appropriately. God confirmed this in my heart once I was willing to let go. "This is not the end, only a delay," He said. "I am doing a work of perfection in you. When I place you with your mate you will see that all these things have taken place so I can be glorified through your lives as a couple. Your testimony will belong to me."

On that note, I submitted myself to spiritual surgery, and a wonderful thing began to happen. First, I chose to put my faith in God. Instead of dictating the specifics, I chose to have faith in who He said He was and what His Word promises He is able to do. Joy began to fill my world as God began to deal with me in different areas in preparation for my mate. He began to point out old wounds and wrong ways of thinking that would affect my marriage. Even old baggage from childhood was brought to my attention! It turned out to be a happy time because I understood the necessity of it. I was excited to know that I was being prepared for my future husband. I had something to look forward to. And so do you!

A little reminder here: Be open to sound and godly counsel. Remember God's blueprint for the man He has chosen for you as we've already discussed. Make sure the voice of reassurance that this man belongs to you is *God's* voice and not your own heart. When we are not ready to receive the truth about our situation, sometimes the cries of our own longings can sound like God. Friends and family may have tried to gently caution us, but we've always had a ready defense for why they don't understand. We need to be willing to hear them. While we are all starry-eyed, they are seeing things in your companion that you don't see. And more often then not, they are right on target. The key to finding out if this really is "your" man is in being willing and able to completely let go. If the man doesn't come back, he isn't God's choice for you. If that is the case, breathe a sigh of relief and say, "Thank You, Lord." You've just been saved from a world of trouble.

Running Away, Running Back

The parable of the prodigal son in Luke 15 doesn't end when he returns home. There was a marked difference in attitude between the father and the prodigal son's older brother, who had stayed at home all along. The faithful son was angry with the father for welcoming his brother back with such overwhelming grace. He was quick to point out what an unappreciative little wretch his brother was for leaving in the first place.

The father, on the other hand, chalked up the younger son's departure as an experience well worth its pain if the boy finally realized that there was no place like home. He understood the humbling that had to take place for the son to return as a brand-new man, able to recognize the value of the things he had taken for granted. The father knew that it was not the time for an "I told you so." The son learned the lesson without any contribution from the father. The bottom line was that he loved his son and knew there was no shame in forgiveness. He seemed to know that the only way his younger son could learn the valuable lessons he needed to learn was through the agony of separation and defeat.

My advice to you, if your man decides to take time off from your relationship, is to let go and let God. Don't be a clinging vine because even the most spiritual man's first inclination is to fight against restrictions. When our hands are open we give God room and full rein to rewrite the poem of our life, a process that cannot be rushed or circumvented.

If this man is, indeed, God's choice for you, despite the spiritual and physical circumstances, you can count on looking down the road and seeing your "Jonah" making his way up the path when you least expect it. And when he returns, he will be a new man. He will have rewritten the script he presented to you earlier. I think you'll like the new ending. His words might go something like this:

> I sit beside you
> > wrapped in thoughtful conversation
> > > feeling too good for comfort . . .
> > the alarm sounds
> > > and my heart awakens
> > > > to ask questions
> > > > > my mind chooses to ignore
> > instead I choose to race with love
> > and I am off and running . . .
> > > oblivious of what I stand to lose
> > or how much I gain
> > > I run from love
> > > > I run from you
> > > > > and become
> > > > > > entangled in
> > > > > > > the echo
> > > > > > > of your laughter . . .
> > > > > > I shake you loose
> > > > > and still I run
> > > > from your voice
> > > from your kiss . . .
> > > > and the wind becomes your touch
> > > > > enveloping me
> > > > > > filling my nostrils
> > > > > > with your scent

and I continue my flight
away from you . . .
running . . .
running for my life
running for the preservation
of my heart . . .
my soul
my mind . . .
running . . .
with my will
tightly clenched
in both hands . . .
I run into my own vulnerability . . .
and for a moment
I'm arrested
by a vision of your eyes . . .
and still I run . . .
until I can run no more . . .
for I am lost . . .
until I find myself
running back to you
back to love . . .

Now what's a woman supposed to do when a man talks like that!

7
The Real Deal

Little girls
   dream of knights on white horses . . .
      but I dream of you
         standing before me
         both feet firmly planted on the ground
  inviting me to ride away with you
  upon the horse
  of high ideals
     and fanciful dreams
       to the land of
         reality and realization . . .

Little girls dream
  of princes
    tenderly kissing their lips
      and gazing into their eyes
        with a lovesick sigh
     but I dream of you
    intense . . .
    and unclouded by illusions
  looking into my eyes
  searching my soul

seeing all of me . . .
    uncovering hidden ground
        finding common ground
    where we meet . . .
        and not even our lips
            stand between us
                for we are one . . .

Little girls
    dream of dragonslayers
        awesome and fearless
            rescuing them
                from dreadful monsters
                    and unseen wizards
                    with dazzling displays
                    of sword mastery . . .
                but I dream of you
            whole, free, and self-assured
        gently turning the key
    and unlocking my emotions . . .
        extending your hand
            and wiping away
                the cobwebs of past hurts . . .
            dispersing suspicious defenses
            breaking the chains of loneliness
        as you introduce me
    to myself . . .
    and you . . .

Little girls
    dream dreams
        that never come true
            but my dreams are
                intermingled
                    with the realness
                        of you . . .

They say that absence makes the heart grow fonder. Well, that sounds very nice and poetic but let's face it, a lot happens in the heart besides fond feelings during separations. Perspectives change; reality sets in. Sometimes when we are entrenched in the depths of a romantic relationship, we are too close to the forest to see the trees. But if we take one step back a whole new wealth of views and attitudes comes into focus. Some are very real, some are exaggerated.

"What if you didn't get a word from the Lord about the man in your life?" you may be asking. "What if you didn't get any kind of feeling about it one way or the other?" If you have not gotten any kind of leading or confirmation in your spirit about this man, my advice to you is to walk softly. Seek the counsel of friends and family that you trust spiritually, as well as your pastor.

If you have no guidance or impression from the Holy Spirit, you need to ask yourself a very important question: Am I pursuing this relationship based on what my flesh wants or what I believe God wants for my life? *If* the man in your life is pulling back from you, the process of his returning may take only a few days, but sometimes it takes longer.

If you are not clear about what this man's position in your life should truly be, you may be trying to hold on to something that doesn't "belong" to you. And just because he may come back to you, it doesn't necessarily mean that he is God's will for you. The Bible describes one case when God gave the Israelites "their request but sent leanness into their soul" (Psalm 106:15). So continue to evaluate boyfriend by God's standards.

Wounds and Bruises

Chapter 5 in Song of Songs tells of the Shulamite woman arising in the night and going in search of her lover. She encounters watchmen in the midst of her seeking. They beat and bruised her and stripped her veil from her. Whenever we choose to venture out in our own flesh, in the dark hours of our lives, our outcomes will be the same as hers. Satan, who roams about as a lion seeking someone to devour, will always be there, ready and willing to take advantage of the fact that we have crept from beneath God's covering. Stepping away from God's covering leaves our hearts open to wounding and bruising. But whether you suffer emotional damage or spiritual degeneration because of your experience, God is able to heal. He promises, "Weeping may endure for a night, but joy comes in the morning" (Psalm 30:5).

The Shulamite woman learned from her experience. The next time she was inclined to go out, she chose to wait until morning before she ventured forth. But, no longer was she in pursuit of her lover! She states that she went "down to the grove of nut trees to look at the new growth in the valley, to see if the vines had budded or the pomegranates were in bloom" (Song of Songs 6:11 NIV). Then, before she realized it, she was surrounded by the chariots of her lover!

She went to look at the new growth in the valley! Like her, we can always count on new growth in the valleys of our lives. This is where the streams of God's grace flow in abundance. As for the vine, Jesus says He is the Master Vine. He asks us to abide in Him. Since you have been grafted into the vine through the spirit of adoption into the family of God, have you attached yourself to Him or have you allowed yourself to wither on the vine and become disconnected from the vine? If you are firmly attached to the vine, the fruit in your life will be rich, succulent, and refreshing like the pomegranate.

Are you seeking after spiritual growth in spite of difficult circumstances? As growth in Him becomes your focus, a pleasant surprise will interrupt your preoccupation with your spiritual maturity. "Before I realized it," the Shulamite woman declared, "my desire set me among the royal chariots of my people" (Song of Songs 6:12). Her godly character attracted this man; he surrounded her.

Proverbs 18:22 states, "He who finds a wife finds a good thing." It is not the other way around. Allow your mate to find you—not just in the sense of physical location, but emotionally and spiritually, too. Make sure you are in a stance of holiness and spiritual maturity when he spots you.

Three Kinds of Beauty

When the Shulamite's lover found her, he could not contain himself; he had to have her. He had to proclaim her beauty to all who would listen. He made note of her beauty on three levels: physically, spiritually, and emotionally.

The first thing he noticed were her feet. Isaiah wrote, "How beautiful upon the mountains are the feet of him who brings good news" (Isaiah 52:7). Scripture also tells us that part of our necessary spiritual armor is having our "feet shod with the preparation of the gospel of peace" (Ephesians 6:15 KJV).

The next thing the lover noticed was her walk—that it was graceful. Do people know that you are a Christian by the way you live your life? Are you growing gracefully in the things of God? Are you dealing graciously with those around you? Is your conversation seasoned with grace?

Her lover then took note of her overall physical beauty. This is still important. Men are visual creatures. No matter how spiritual you are, packaging still counts. (We'll talk more about that later.) The Shulamite's lover didn't stop with her physical beauty. He went on to comment on her emotional beauty—the fruit her life bore and how it affected those around her, including him. His words to her were, "How beautiful you are, and how pleasing, O love, with your delights!" (Song of Songs 7:6 NIV).

In the face of all these compliments and praise, the Shulamite woman retained her well-kept status and did not become intoxicated by his adoration. Her heart was fixed and her mind made up to focus on being God's woman first, the man's woman second. She gracefully acknowledged, "I belong to my lover, and his desire is for me," but then she quickly set the tone for their relationship. She encouraged, "Let us get up early to the vineyards; let us see if the vine has budded, whether the grape blossoms are open and the pomegranates are in bloom. There I will give you my love" (Song of Songs 7:12). There was a condition to her giving her heart over totally.

This woman had spent time allowing God to groom her for this moment. He had grounded her in His reality. No matter how much she longed for a mate, no matter how much she liked him, no matter how much she wanted to elope upon his proclamation of his undying love for her, she was not going to budge until she examined the fruit of his life and the fruit of their relationship.

She again reinforced her resolve. "Do not stir up nor awaken love until it pleases" (Song of Songs 8:4). She had to be sure that their relationship would promote continued spiritual growth, not moral decay. Is this a detail we tend to overlook in our relationships? Continued spiritual growth is the real deal. That is maturity. That is sound reasoning. That is the foundation of your relationship—a foundation that can weather the storms of relationship.

In Search of Clear Vision

Are you seeing the man in your life as he really is? Or are you like the man who went to Jesus to have his sight restored? (See Mark 4:23-25.) First, Jesus lead him out of the village. He then touched his eyes and asked him what he saw. The man replied, "I see men as trees." Of course, Jesus would not leave him in that state. He touched the man's eyes again, and this time his sight was restored and he saw clearly. Jesus then sent him home, cautioning him not to go into the village. I found that interesting. Was there something in the village that had affected his sight? Is your relationship or your surroundings affecting your focus?

The first point is that the blind man went to Jesus. Are you still seeking Him? We need to make sure we can say, "Jesus is still first in our lives."

Second, we need to make sure we're focusing correctly— that we're not seeing "men as trees," but really seeing them as they are. We need to affirm that "yes, I have examined my partner's walk with the Lord, and have made an accurate evaluation of our spiritual growth together. I have judged it to be progressing in a manner I feel would be pleasing to God."

Third, we need to be sure that we are surrounding ourselves with God's love and wisdom, so we can proclaim, "Yes, I have confirmation in my spirit that this is the man God has chosen for me to share my life with and lend my support to."

Now that we see our relationship through God's perspective, what about our human reactions?

Living with Imperfections

When you notice that pimple on his nose, do you decide he's totally ugly?—or do you see a nice face with a pimple on it? Usually after taking a step back or having a short separation from the man of our affections, our sense of reality swings like a pendulum. Our perception of truth can become exaggerated, and things may appear to be worse than they are.

Just because we've done away with the fairy-tale ideas and the fanciful notions detailed in the poem at the beginning of this chapter, that doesn't mean we've arrived. Whether we choose to admit it or not, when we first started seeing Mr. Right, we probably couldn't think of one thing about him that we would change. Even his weaknesses were cute!

Now those same things that you found cute have you concerned. The pendulum has swung from ignoring and accepting everything about this person to ruthlessly scrutinizing every minute detail and demanding that he line up to absolute perfection. For those of you who did not go through the separation dilemma we discussed earlier, this begins to occur as you get used to the person being around consistently. The rose-colored glasses come off, and we're off and running with a full list of complaints and reconsiderations of this poor, unsuspecting man.

It has been said that women tend to major in minors, while men check out the whole picture, deal with things at face value, and accept what they can't change (at least in the courtship stage). The things we find important are not as important to them.

Before you voice your complaints, observations, and reservations, I urge you to allow God to balance your reality. We will take a closer look at this later, but for now I urge you to not allow the things you see to cause you to make decisions in the flesh without submitting your concerns to God. After all, only God knows what this man sees when he looks at you!

What Has Really Been Promised?

Seeing your boyfriend clearly is important, but not just to collect information to figure out if you really want to put up with this person or not. The revelations you receive about this person are for the same purpose as the ones you receive about yourself. They are for you to pray over and, perhaps, grow in that area. With the leading of the Holy Spirit, render yourself useful by praying for your man in the area that's been pointed out to you. Let me make myself perfectly clear. I am not referring to serious, questionable character traits or dysfunctional behavior. I am talking about unrealistic and self-righteous judgments (usually inspired by fear) we make in overly critical examinations. It is God who works changes in people, and only if He wants things changed. Maybe some of the things you don't like are revealing something in you that needs to be changed!

Fortunately, God isn't in the business of discarding us even though He sees the reality of who we are. He doesn't allow us to use the fact that we are human as an excuse, either. He simply covers our sorry realities with the blood of His Son, Jesus, and gently takes us through a reformation program designed, timed, and orchestrated by the Holy Spirit. We have to be willing to allow Him to do the same with the other people in our lives.

And remember, as quiet as it's kept, boyfriend is already panicking. He's trying to figure out how he's going to keep up your image of him as your fantasy-come-to-life. (No, he doesn't realize that he's already blown his cover.) If he had the courage, this is what he would tell you:

I can't promise you
    cloudless skies
        continual bliss
            or thornless rose gardens . . .

I can't promise you
    painless days
        tearless nights
            or even endless passion
                for I've already promised you
                truth . . .

I can't promise you
    the stuff
        movies and romance novels
            are made of . . .
                momentary wishes
                dreams come true . . .
            or the thrill of a lifetime . . .
        for I've already
    promised you reality . . .

I can't promise you
    world fortunes
        conquered empires
            or trips to the moon . . .
                for I've already promised you
                all that I have . . .

I can't promise you
    answers for every question
        freedom from fear
            or a brand-new day . . .
                because promises of everything
            usually add up to nothing . . .
        and I've already promised
    not to make promises
I can't keep . . .
    therefore . . .
        all I can promise you
            is me . . .

8
Confrontation

Before I begin I must admit that this is probably the hardest chapter of this book for me to write. Confrontation, no matter which angle I view it from, always towers in front of me as a mountain I would rather not climb. No matter how spectacular the view promises to be from the top, fear of falling, breaking a nail, messing up my hair, or—God forbid—smudging my makeup, loom as enormous threats to me. Whether confronting or being confronted, I immediately break out in a sweat. I know in either case I'm going to be forced to deal with my worse enemy . . . me.

Our God is a confrontational God. He is much more concerned about our lives than our nails. And when He holds up His Holy Ghost mirror to your soul—or mine—no matter how gently he does it our initial reaction may be to scream and run away. Of course we can refuse to look at and deal honestly with what we see, but that involves the risk of going through life thinking we're looking marvelous and charming the world, only to find that at the end of the evening we've had a piece of green vegetable stuck between our teeth the whole time. Or, even more embarrassing, we've been trailing toilet paper on our classic Chanel pumps. Let me illustrate through a personal example.

A Cycle of Mistakes

One night I had a most disturbing dream. I was at a flea market with a friend of mine. As we walked among all the gaudy treasures, I was telling her all about another friend's engagement ring, which had to total at least nine carats minimum. As I described the ring I was waving my hands in excitement. Much to my surprise, I realized I had the ring on! Somehow I had tried on the ring and never returned it to my friend.

Suddenly I got distracted by a tray of costume jewelry and dove into it with delight. In the midst of my looking, the center stone in the ring I was wearing loosened and fell into the bin and got lost among all the junk jewelry. As frantically as I searched, I was unable to find the stone, unable to discern the real diamond from the paste ones.

Well, you can imagine my consternation when I woke up. Since I'm prone to argue with the truth when I'm awake, God often deals with me through dreams when I'm sleeping. As soon as I woke up, I did what any truly spiritual person would do. I sought the Lord for the interpretation. What he revealed was sobering.

The Lord showed me that, yes, I wanted the real thing, and rejoiced when others found the real thing. But when it came to my own personal choices, I had trouble recognizing what the real thing was. I had grown so used to counterfeits that they had become the norm. I was unable to value the real thing and treat it with the care that it deserved. If I continued on in ignorance, I was in danger of losing real love, even if I managed to grasp it for a time.

Like me, have you found yourself going around in circles, making the same mistakes over and over again? I laughingly told a friend one day that I knew I had dated the same man too many times to count. He had appeared in different sizes, shapes, and colors—different men, same story.

It may have been a cute joke, but it was a sad commentary on my all-too-real life. I was always attracted to men who needed me. I would nurse and mother them; they would get well and go off in search of a woman to be their wife, not their mother. Many of them became spiritual powerhouses (thanks, I'm sure, to my maternal touch), and though I'm sure God was quite pleased, I felt it was about time I got some personal gratification out of this repetitive cycle!

Turning on the Lights

While complaining to a male friend of mine one day, he said, "You don't really want to get married because, if you did, you would make different choices, and you would be married by now. Nothing is wrong with you, it's the men you choose to get involved with."

His words left me speechless, and, honey, that takes a lot. How could I have overlooked this very simple fact? What was it in me that drew me into the same episode of the same disappointing soap opera time and time again? I had a blind spot, and Satan knew it. And with this dangerous piece of information in his hands, Satan played on it.

The Word of God says that Satan comes to steal, kill, and destroy. He comes to steal the promises and blessings of God from your life. He is determined to kill your faith and joy. And he won't be satisfied until he has destroyed your relationships on three levels—with God, with yourself (your self-esteem), and with other people. This crafty, devious troublemaker revels in our blind spots, and dances a delighted jig when we crash. He leaves us lying in the debris of our shattered hopes and dreams, mad at God, mad at ourselves, and bitter toward others.

But there's One who knows the truth. When He decides it's time to take our lives to another level, He turns on the light exposing the darkness, the blind spots, the hidden things in our hearts that keep us in bondage to past mistakes and hindrances. Some say the truth hurts. But in reality the truth will set us free—if, that is, we take responsibility for it. Truth must be acknowledged and accepted. Then comes a yielding to God's power to work a transformation in us. Out of the surrender comes the blessing, the performance of all that God has promised us, the answers to the secret cries of our hearts.

Let's take a look at three more Bible passages that tell us something about God's best intentions for us and reveal the challenges we face when we come to terms with ourselves—and one of which poses a "giant" threat we must confront (more about that in a minute).

The First Couple

I love to reflect upon Adam as he walked and talked with God and tended the garden. The Lord God said, "It is not good for the man to be alone. I will make a helper suitable for him" (NIV). In Genesis 2:19-24 (NIV) we read,

> Now the LORD God had formed out of the ground all the beasts of the field and all the birds of the air. He brought them to the man to see what he would name them; and whatever the man called each living creature, that was its name. So the man gave names to all the livestock, the birds of the air and all the beasts of the field. But for Adam no suitable helper was found.
>
> So the LORD God caused the man to fall into a deep sleep; and while he was sleeping, he took one of the man's ribs and closed up the place with flesh. Then the LORD God made a woman from the rib he had taken out of the man, and he brought her to the man. The man said, "This is now bone of my bones and flesh of my flesh; she shall be called 'woman,' for she was taken out of man." For this reason a man will leave his father and mother and be united to his wife, and they will become one flesh.

Many times, I've read this passage and come away with one nugget: Woman was made from man. But now, other things are evident. Let's briefly outline the facts. First, God said it wasn't good for man to be alone. We can all agree with that! Then He brought all the animals to Adam to see what he would name them. This was what really caught my attention, because it's followed by this phrase—but for Adam no suitable helper was found.

Was Adam supposed to find his mate among the animals? Since no word written in the Word of God should be taken for granted, this series of events must be scrutinized more closely. Why did God have Adam name all the animals before presenting him with his mate? In His foreknowledge, why did he want to see what Adam would name them? Since God created all things, wasn't it also His right to name them?

After meditating on these questions, I've come to several conclusions. The first one is that Adam and God had such a close fellowship that Adam initially was not aware that anything was missing, that he needed anyone or anything but God and the provisions He provided. When God brought the animals to Adam for a closer look before the great naming ceremony began, I think Adam finally noticed that there were male and female of everything—made for one another! It must have been a startling revelation.

The Perfect Match

In my mind's eye I can picture the scene. "Like kind" was joined to "like kind." This stirred something in Adam. He began to search, to see if "his kind" had somehow slipped past him in previous rounds through the garden. But of all he saw, and all he named, there was no one like him. No one else spoke his language nor had the same heartbeat. No match fit him perfectly. There were lots of beautiful options, but nothing quite fit the bill.

So God caused him to fall asleep and fashioned a woman out of his own flesh. A perfect complement. A twin reflection of himself—with a couple of minor adjustments. When Adam woke up, he probably thought, "Now this is more like it!"

Instinctively he knew that this was a personal gift from God. She was made to order, made to fit him like a hand in a glove. And for this reason he was joined to her, and they walked as one, in perfect coexistence (until they fell into sin, but that's another story).

What am I trying to say here? Simply this: I think we've all been through several naming ceremonies, and we've handed out a lot of wrong names, such as:

- "Mr. Perfect-for-Me"
- "Mr. My-Type"
- "Mr. Dream-Man"
- "Mr. He'll-Do-I-Just-Need-to-Fix-Him-Up-a-Bit"
- "Mr. After-Waiting-So-Long-I-Can-Live-with-This"
- "Mr. I-Can't-Take-Another-Day-Alone-I'll-Take-Him."

Some of us have given a lot of men the coveted title of "life-mate," a title that should have been reserved for the ones God made specially for us.

I believe it was clear to Adam, after naming all the animals, after seeing how beautiful they all were, that it would not be beneficial for him to try to force a match. He knew himself, his needs, his desires, his strengths, his weaknesses, and he knew God. So after quite a bit of thought, and a discussion with God about his findings, God said, "Hey, just chill, I've got something for you!" With that, Adam trustingly laid himself in the arms of God and allowed Him to fashion one of His finest creations (if I do say so myself)—woman.

As we lay ourselves trustingly in the arms of God, how can we discern which man He has created for us? How can we know who to embrace and who to avoid? Let's start by taking inventory. First, make a list of all the people you've dated or been interested in. Next make a brief outline of what happened in each relationship or encounter. Then make another column and list the similarities or the common thread that ran through each relationship. Now, make a list of your attitude and behavior in each case. If you have difficulty doing this and are having a hard time being objective, ask your friends what they have observed with regard to your love interests.

This could prove to be a painful exercise, but if you're truly sick and tired of being sick and tired of failed relationships, you will take every step necessary to be free and in position for God's blessing. The first step to recovery is admitting exactly who you are and where you are. Look in the mirror. Take off the makeup and be honest about what you really see. What are you? Who are you? You won't be the first person to take a hard look at yourself, and you won't be the last. You will survive, as proven by some very high profile predecessors.

How to Get a New Name

I love the story in Genesis about Jacob. This man was something else! His name, which means "manipulator," even warned people to look out. He was, in fact, a master manipulator. This character flaw paved the way for him to become a victim of the same thing that he dished out (which is usually what happens). God will always make sure there is someone in our lives who mirrors our character traits. This person usually becomes a major source of irritation because you are reminded of the effect your own actions have on others.

When Jacob finally grew weary of manipulating and being manipulated, he found himself in the middle of the night, in the middle of nowhere, duking it out with an angel of the Lord! So determined was Jacob to get past where he was stuck, he dared, while hanging on for dear life, to say to the Lord, "I won't let go until You bless me!"

In response to this defiant resolution, the Lord asked, "What is your name?"

"Jacob," he answered.

Then the Lord told him, "Your name will no longer be Jacob, but Israel, because you have struggled with God and with men and have overcome." (See Genesis 32:22-28.)

Because Jacob was able to be honest and state who he was, and what he was really made of, a change took place. God was able to do a work of transformation in Jacob's life so dramatic that his name had to be changed! Jacob no longer was "manipulator," but Israel, "he struggles with God." As the sun rose the next morning after this life-changing encounter, Jacob was walking with a limp—the struggle had crippled him—but he was a new man as he went back to face a difficult situation he had created in his unregenerated state. And because he was a different man, a potentially volatile encounter was resolved in peace.

Jacob and his brother, Esau, had parted under very hostile conditions. Now, after owning up to who he was and what he was really made of, Jacob used godly wisdom and the two were peaceably reunited. What could have been a catastrophe became a turning point of Jacob's life, and he was able to continue on his way without further incident.

Jacob didn't blame God for his bad choices or for the problems they left behind for him to deal with. Neither should we. God isn't responsible for our mistakes. In this life, we will have many temptations. We will be tempted by our own desires, but God has promised to make a way of escape from every temptation.

The blame game is not conducive to kingdom living. Seldom do people get anywhere in any area of life if they refuse to deal with themselves. Fortunately, we have a Father who loves us, who will not condone or allow us to get away with this sort of irresponsible behavior. This is why He allows valley, desert, and wilderness experiences. Each provides different circumstances and produces different fruit in us.

Valley, Desert, and Wilderness Wanderings

The valley is a low place filled with sorrow and intense loneliness. It is also a place where rivers flow down from the mountains, making the earth rich with abundant vegetation—with the fruit of the Holy Spirit.

The desert is a vast, dry place with no relief from the heat. It is where your mind will play tricks on you, and you will come face-to-face with the devil and face-to-face with God. A place where you will make a stand for one or fall for the other, depending on your convictions.

And then there is the wilderness, filled with endless wandering, fear, and unbelief. God allowed the Israelites to wander in the wilderness for 40 years. Why? To humble them and test them in order to know what was in their hearts.

The pressure of uncertainty and what we consider deprivation will either make us bow to idols or lay prostrate before a holy and awesome God awaiting direction. In the wilderness, we can make one of two choices. We can remain in a place of unfulfillment, aimlessly wandering, discontentedly murmuring against God and blaming Him for our lot in life. Or we can choose to forcefully move forward in anticipation of claiming His promises for our lives.

Dealing with Giants

It is a general principle that for every promise claimed a giant must be slain. When Jacob wrestled with the angel of the Lord, the giants within him were being slain. And there are giants inside all of us.

Some giants are loud, boisterous, and accusing like Goliath. The threats they level at us leave us paralyzed and afraid to fight. In response, we dig deeper trenches for ourselves, burrowing in, listening to the empty lies that somehow seem true and insurmountable in our ears:

"You'll never get married."

"You aren't capable of having a fulfilling relationship."

"You're too fat."

"You're too thin."

"If only your personality were different."

On and on these "giant" lies continue. As we accept their verdicts as facts, we die quietly and sorrowfully.

Then there are the sleeping giants. We are not aware that they exist until we intrude on their space, trespass on their territory, or faint in the midst of a battle. Then they spring up and try to intimidate and terrorize us, to make us turn back from the promises of God.

The land of love has been prepared for us, but there are giants there. Love has been promised to every believer, whether it be love for a dying world, for a special mate, or for a newborn child. God wants you to feel how His heart beats for you. And only in the land of love will you discover the complete richness of His character and how much He cares for you. Only in this place will you be able to understand why He was willing to sacrifice His own Son for the sake of reconciliation with you. You will never understand a love that strong until you've given it yourself.

Entering the Land of Love

No wonder the enemy makes it so difficult for us to enter into love. No wonder he places giants in our way. The power that comes from love's discovery is transformative, and one transformed life changes other lives and glorifies the Father. Everything that happens to us always comes back, full circle, to God's purpose being fulfilled.

Yes, there are giants in the land. But this reality should not make us settle for the leeks, onions, and hopeless relationships in Egypt. Decide that you are willing to fight for what is rightfully yours. Make up your mind that you won't let go until God blesses you. You must be willing to look your soul's giants straight in the eye and then slay them. As He helped David kill Goliath with a single blow to the head, God will help you. But He seeks your cooperation. Look in the mirror of your soul and ask God to expose everything in you that He wants to fix in preparation for that glorious procession into the promised land.

I have one final warning about entering the land of promise. The Israelites were upset with the news about giants because, in essence, it meant taking off their rose-colored glasses. They expected everything to be easy and painless. But God knows that a smooth path does little to promote growth or dependency on Him.

You will know you're ready to enter the land of love when you see everything as it really is. When you understand the commitment marriage really calls for, and what your mate and God will expect from you. The land of promise is also a land of responsibility and total surrender. I hope and pray you're willing to do whatever it takes (whether it be wrestling some personal giants or putting love-threatening habits to death) to be totally equipped to answer the challenge to enter the land of love.

> *Love calls me to come outside*
> *leaving the comfort zone*
> *of my own selfishness*
> *and protective fortresses behind*
> *to discover your needs*
> *before my own*
> *to find my fulfillment*
> *lies hidden*
> *in the exchange of I for us . . .*
>
> *Love calls and I answer*
> *tentatively treading on uncertain ground*
> *testing its ability*
> *to bear the weight of my heart*
> *and my expectations*
> *fear of falling*
> *causing me to love gingerly . . .*
> *holding my breath*
> *I take a chance*
> *on losing myself in you*
> *pleasantly surprised*
> *to find you so generous*
> *with your tenderness*
> *your secret places*
> *putting your trust in my hands . . .*

I stand ashamed
of all that I still withhold from you
and I am challenged
to forsake everything that I consider safe . . .

Love calls
and my yearning
races ahead of my suspicious will . . .
throwing caution to the wind
I release all that I am
only to find
that I've lost nothing
and found everything
in the discovery
that the real comfort zone
is in your arms . . .

9
The Truth Comes Out

Jesus said, "You shall know the truth, and the truth shall make you free." In more modern days, someone added, "But it'll hurt first." This is true. Let's take a deeper look at patterns and habits that can sabotage our most promising relationships.

A Family Affair

When it comes to relationships, you would be surprised at how much you may unconsciously mimic the actions of your parents and family members. The environment you grew up in is a representation of the normal world to you. Whether your home environment was troubled or not, you got used to feeling a certain way. Anything else beyond your usual experience becomes unfamiliar and uncomfortable—even if it's good!

A common joke in our society centers around how girls marry younger versions of their fathers, and young men marry younger versions of their mothers. It's so true. Even if you had a horrible relationship with your father, chances are you will end up marrying someone who is much like him (unless, of course, you've allowed God to heal the hurt). And you'll keep trying to "fix him." Sadly, most of the time this is a fruitless exercise.

I'm sure that after Jacob had his life-altering wrestling match with God and realized all the mistakes he had made in his life, he tried to impart this knowledge to his children. But by then, they were already swirling with activity and were unwilling to listen. Instead, they were drowning in the sea of their own justifications for their blind and costly actions.

Brotherly Love

Once Jacob had received his new name, Israel, and had seen 12 sons born to him, you'd think he would have been spared some difficulty. But most of his sons were just as devious as he had been when he was younger.

Once his favorite wife, Rachel, died, Israel showered all his grief and love onto her firstborn son, Joseph. Meanwhile, Joseph's half-brothers were growing more and more jealous of their younger sibling. So while Joseph dreamed, his brothers schemed his demise. They finally ended up selling him down the river, into slavery in Egypt. As far as the brothers were concerned, Joseph was out of sight, out of mind. As far as his poor old father knew, Joseph was dead.

Here's where God's wonderful sense of humor comes into play. After years of battling their own guilt, guess who the brothers had to face in order to get food when famine hit the land? None other than long-lost Joseph! They were suddenly forced to look into the eyes of their own deceitfulness and see the need to repent. In God's providence and sovereign plan He had preserved Joseph's life in Egypt and promoted him to high station. The hand that the brothers had taken such pleasure in biting was now the hand that would—or wouldn't—feed them. If Joseph's story is not an example of how the enemy can subtly weave his mess through a family tree, I don't know what is.

Ties That Bind Us

Only God can break the chains that bind us to the unhealthy actions of our family. Only He can sever generational bondages and spiritual oppression (the kind that come from the "iniquity of the fathers being visited upon the children unto the third and fourth generation"). The saying that "those who forget their history are destined to repeat it" is true. Family mistakes that go unsurrendered to the Lord have a tendency to resurface from generation to generation. Fortunately for Israel's manipulative sons, Joseph was a godly man who forgave his brothers and made a home for them in Egypt. Some families are less forgiving.

The words, "I'll *never* be like my mother or father" have gotten a lot of people in trouble. Vows such as this place us in greater bondage than we can imagine. When we focus on the faults of others we stand in danger of becoming like them. We begin to develop the root traits of that person. For example, this is why the child of an alcoholic might not drink, but may develop an addiction in another area. The addiction may be different, but the root attitude is the same. Forgiveness and releasing *anyone* who has offended us is of monumental importance. This is the road to freedom and good health.

Of course, there are less obvious areas of spiritual oppression that can wreak havoc among the unsuspecting for generations. Slavery, for example, was one of the catalysts for great spiritual oppression that is still pervasive in many African-American families. The enemy has woven subtle patterns of defeat into the fabric of male-female relationships, and the children are caught in the crossfire. Angry and confused, they retrace a pattern they don't even understand.

When slave masters sold off the men and broke up their families, a pattern of thinking that it was normal to leave was established. When the women could not be protected by their men from the atrocities of slavery, such as rape, separation from their children, the humiliation of being treated like property, they began to believe the lies of their "masters" that their men were "no good." The enemy influenced them to become cold and tough in order to survive.

After a while, African-American women didn't know how to let go and let a man be a man in their lives anymore. They repeated the lies of the slave master, and they taught their children to believe as they did. The men, confused and broken in spirit, gave up the fight and settled for living up to the accusations—a vicious cycle that still impacts society. Of course, many things have contributed to the further proliferation of this problem, but the enemy can still be found lurking beneath the surface of it all.

The light must be shed on the enemy's tactics. The smoke screen must be dispersed, and the truth clearly revealed.

Angels of Light

Since Satan's main method of operation is to come "disguised as an angel of light," he usually dresses the deception he places in our lives in beautiful packages. He is acutely aware of our blind spots and uses them artfully. He has probably kept a file on you. Since he is not omnipresent like God, he may well have assigned to you a spiritual adversary, to watch and report your every move, your every mistake, your every weakness.

Keeping you oblivious or in denial of your own personal pitfalls is essential to the enemy if he is to succeed at keeping you unvictorious in life. He takes advantage of the things he knows that you don't. When you refuse to look in the mirror of truth the Holy Spirit extends to you, Satan rejoices because he is well aware of your ignorance. And his gain is your loss.

This is why it is important to continually ask God for revelation when we find ourselves caught up in destructive patterns. Just in case it's not so obvious, I highly recommend asking God to reveal to you the self-defeating behaviors of which you may not be aware. If you are in denial because you feel too overwhelmed to break the undesirable chain of events in your life, now is the time to face the music and do a freedom dance. Now is the time to get on with the rest of your life. When you finally decide you are ready to move on, you'll work as hard as possible to get free.

In my own life, my weakness was the men I chose. I gravitated toward emotionally selfish men. They all were so handsome, witty, interesting, and romantic that I failed to notice they were unwilling or incapable of making a commitment. Do you remember the man I told you about earlier, the one that had reduced me to attending a tea party with the enemy? After three years of refusing to speak to him, struggling to recover, and finally being able to remove the last bandage from my heart, you'll never believe what happened. He resurfaced—divorced and saved! How do you like that? Just when I was getting myself together he shows up.

He was quite eager to reestablish a friendship. He filled my world with wonderful phone calls, loads of attention, and indulgent gifts. I enjoyed all of the attention and found myself unconsciously slipping into the same warm, fuzzy place I had enjoyed with this man before. But this time I had some reservations. I wasn't sure where I wanted the relationship to go. Gradually I was becoming more aware of my weaknesses. I was beginning to look in the mirror. Although painful, this was good, because it soon became apparent that this man still wasn't willing to make a commitment to me. That's when it really hit me that something was very wrong.

I began to realize that unpromising situations were a little too easy for me to fall into. They were a little too comfortable. I was becoming aware of the truth, of my blind spot: My consistent pattern of attraction always set me up for rejection and disappointment. Was this pattern followed so I could feel relieved when things finally fell apart? Or was I caught up in the drama of expressing how hurt I was? Sometimes it was hard to tell. But I finally made a startling discovery, thanks to my friend the Holy Spirit: I associated love with longing.

Daddies' Girl

I am especially fortunate in the respect that I have two fathers. (I don't think of my mother's second husband as a stepfather because he was always a true father to me.) Even though my natural father and my second father are two very different men, they both had the exact same effect on my emotions and my spirit.

My natural father lived overseas. I was reunited with him at the age of 14 after 12 years of separation. As a child I had longed to know him, and as a young woman, I longed to spend more time with him.

My other father, whom I affectionately call "Poppa Do," would do anything for me, but he's a man of few words. I wanted him to be more talkative and overt to fill my need for connection. Both of my fathers are strict disciplinarians, yet indulgent when it comes to anything I wanted or needed. They are both wonderful men that I love dearly and am very proud to have as parents. I'm sure they both did the best they could, in light of their knowledge and experience. But both were, in my arena of need, either physically or emotionally remote. I was always yearning for more of them. Therefore, "longing" became a "normal" feeling to me.

Because of this unmet need, I had countless long distance relationships with men, one right after the other. My friends noticed this destructive pattern, but I didn't understand what the problem was. I thought distance made the relationship more interesting because it was so great to finally see a man after missing him for a while. I felt the situation helped me really appreciate him. Meanwhile, when men approached me who were intent on nailing down a commitment, I fled. Consistent, close commitment wasn't part of my "normal." It scared me, even though I was always screaming that a permanent, committed relationship was what I really wanted. What was my problem?

Men who were able to commit were boring to me; they weren't "my type." On the other hand, in retrospect, I can see that the men I rejected had more of the qualities I really wanted in a life companion than the men I gravitated toward. I would catch myself wondering why I wasn't able to be interested in them, shaking my head at the irony of it all, and moving on in pursuit of a suitor who would make me work to earn his attention and declarations of love. I was still trying to "fix" my relationships with my fathers. I was like a poor person who had won the lottery and having to unload the blessing because I wasn't used to the freedom it brought.

After Moses had led the people out of captivity, the Israelites started complaining because the way to freedom was difficult. They didn't grasp the concept of the promised land so they became discouraged and spoke of returning to Egypt and slavery, where their needs were provided for. They wanted to return to their "normal."

Like them, I preferred the land of Egypt in my heart. I had no concept of the promised land and the thought of living there made me nervous. I was choosing to make bricks without any straw. At least I already knew the end result, and there would be no surprises.

Help from Above

This is familiar territory to far more women than we can count. The saying, "You always want what you can't have" seems to roll off our tongues way too easily. Did it start in the garden of Eden? Adam and Eve had been given permission to eat of every tree in the garden except one, and they had to get stuck on that one, thanks to a little inspiration from a slimy snake. Could it be that the same slippery little snake still enjoys extending invitations to sample fruit we shouldn't be eating? Does the pursuit of happiness really have to be so hard? No, no, a thousand times, no!

God wants all of our relationships to be healthy, comfortable ones. We need to submit every need, every want, every burden, every care to Him. As He begins the healing and deliverance process in us, we become whole, healthy, and lovable.

When we cast off ignorance and denial and let Him fill all of the empty places in us, we become women who will not settle for relationships and situations that are not conducive to our well-being. We will no longer be conformed to the pattern of the world because of past experiences and generational bondages. Instead, we will be "transformed by the renewing of our minds" as we learn about God's perfect love and what is considered "normal" to Him.

Once you've taken the time to allow God to work out whatever the love-hindering issue was (or is) in your life, word will get back to Satan that his secret is out, and he has been defeated. He will have to retreat in order to come up with some other trick to throw you off the scent of victory. Gradually, you will begin to attract, and be attracted to a different type of man. As you walk in freedom and wholeness you will be sending off silent signals that announce . . .

> *I want a man*
> > *not just any man*
> > > *I want God's man*
> > > > *hand-picked*
> > > > > *kingdom appointed*
> > > > > > *for such a woman as this . . .*

> *I'm looking for a love*
> > *not just any love*
> > > *I want the God kind of love*
> > > > *filling a heart that beats*
> > > > > *to the kingdom's rhythm*
> > > > > > *unadulterated*
> > > > > > *Holy Ghost saturated*
> > > > > *the kinda love that*
> > > > *can't be rated . . .*
> > > > > *poured out*
> > > > > > *runnin' ovah*
> > > > > > > *like water in a glass*
> > > > > > *already full of good things*
> > > > > *smooth as silk*
> > > > *yet tough as rope*
> > > *wrapping around my soul*
> > > > *keepin' it all together*
> > > > > *forever*

with room enough for me
to be
a woman
not just any woman
God's woman
whole and free
to love you
the way I want you to love me
with a love
not just any love
but the God kind of love
rich as a sinful dessert
pure as tried gold
the kind of love that can hold
onto your hand
and God's at the very same time
delivered from all other ties that bind
and yes
I'm free enough to wait . . .
for a man
not just any man
but the man
who understands
and knows what love means
and lives what God says . . .
and wants what I want
a real love
a strong love
a tall love
agape love.
God's love.

10
Truth or Consequences

"That's just the way I am!"

"My partner should take me as I am or not at all!"

"If I have to change, I'd rather be alone!"

If these words sound vaguely familiar, you may be stuck in certain patterns of behavior that are destroying your relationships . . . and you may be turning a deaf ear to correction.

When we refuse to change, we refuse to grow. And God expects His children to grow. If you find yourself making the same mistakes again and again, you may be refusing to allow God to transform you. Whether we want to acknowledge it or not, He has set certain spiritual ground rules or universal laws in place for our lives. The world calls it cause and effect. Whatever the name, the results are the same. The moment you violate one of God's principles, no matter how sincere or well-intentioned you were, a consequence kicks in.

Priceless Spiritual Boundaries

These ground rules and their consequences aren't a form of divine manipulation. They are loving boundaries meant to keep you in your rightful role, a role that God ordained for your personal benefit, protection, and blessing. Here's a classic example:

Men flee when women pursue them. Men were created to pursue. It's in their nature. Remember Proverbs 18:22: "He who finds a wife finds what is a good thing."

In some cases, men don't even know why they're running, they're just being true to their spiritual nature. Many things that seem quite innocent and well-intentioned, that seem okay in today's society, can backfire and stall your love-mobile before you get out of the driveway.

There are certain disciplines that must be observed so your journey on the highway of love doesn't end in a sudden crash or, worse yet, a massive pileup of repeated mistakes and serious injuries. I'm pretty certain there were friends and loved ones holding up flashing-yellow caution lights along the roadside of your last trip. But, in the euphoria of the moment, you stepped on the gas, refused to shift gears, slow down, or change direction. You were convinced that you would reach your destination.

We do ourselves a serious disservice when we refuse to at least consider the cautions and observations of those who love us. God's Word (NIV) says:

> Whoever loves discipline loves knowledge, but [she] who hates correction is stupid (Proverbs 12:1).

> [She] who ignores discipline comes to poverty and shame, but whoever heeds correction is honored (Proverbs 13:18).

> [She] who ignores discipline despises [herself], but whoever heeds correction gains understanding (Proverbs 15:32).

Let's face it, we've heard it all. We've read every book, listened to every speaker on every talk show. Most of us could probably conduct our own seminars based on all the information we've compiled. Yet we remain unvictorious in this one area of life. Why? Because head knowledge is not enough: "Get wisdom. And in all your getting, get understanding" (Proverbs 4:7).

Please remember that, first and foremost, God's purpose and timing are serious factors when it comes to getting to the church on time. Preparing for that day requires more than selecting a dress. While we cannot hinder God's purpose, we can actively assist Satan in delaying its arrival. That's what happens when we don't yield to our loving Father's instruction, which often comes to us by way of concerned friends and family members. Stop flying into a tailspin every time someone points out a self-defeating choice or action you've made!

Moments of truth with a good friend may cut deep into your pride, but remember, the "wounds from a friend can be trusted, but an enemy multiplies kisses" (Proverbs 27:6 NIV). And besides, your friend is probably confirming what the Holy Spirit has been trying to tell you anyway. So deal with it! If I may paraphrase, "Be a doer of the truth and not a hearer only, deceiving yourself. Because if you are a hearer of the truth, and not a doer, you are like a person who sees her face in a mirror, and after looking at herself, goes away and immediately forgets what she looks like. But the person who intently pays attention to the truth that gives freedom, not forgetting what she's heard and practicing it, will be blessed in whatever she does" (see James 1:22-25). Sounds good to me!

Samson: What *Not* to Do!

There's a character in Scripture who made a lot of major mistakes and never learned a thing. Remember Samson? The fine dude with the Arnold Schwartzenegger body and the long, flowing locks? Samson started off well enough, but somewhere along the way he got tired of being good. He decided to liven things up a little.

The first thing he did was start hanging out in the wrong places. Ring any bells, ladies? Now you and I know there are certain places where one meets many people who should not and cannot be taken seriously. Anyway, Samson went down to Timnah. Two directions are made clear in that statement. First, the word down indicates that Samson was on a spiritual decline.

Second, "to Timnah" describes foreign territory, the land of the enemy.

"What was he thinking!" we exclaim. Don't get too uppity. He was thinking the same thing we're thinking when we're in the same situation: "I'm bored; I'm tired of waiting for God to make a move." These famous last words are usually spoken as you head off to a singles bar or somewhere just as foolish and unproductive.

Like Samson, you may be conducting your manhunt in an unwholesome fashion and rationalizing your excursions. You're only hunting within Christian circles, but you're dashing from church to church, from singles group to singles group, hoping to catch the scent of eligible Christian men. Stop it! Remember—you are not looking for *any* man. You are waiting for *the* man—the one God has selected for you.

Maybe you believe there's more than one man who could be your possible mate. I won't argue with you, but the bottom line is still the same: You only need one. If you had a choice of five men, you wouldn't settle for saying "eeny, meeny, miny, mo." Logic suggests that one of those men is a better choice than the others. Would you be able to figure out which was the best one without the help of the Holy Spirit? I don't think so. All the more cause to sit down and take a chill pill. God knows your address. He knows your schedule, your goings, and your comings. He is the great matchmaker. He knows how to orchestrate meetings between people.

So take a deep breath and repeat after me, "It's the *man* who finds a good thing, it's the *man* who finds a good thing." Keep saying it until it gets past your head and into your heart. There, doesn't that feel better? It's a relief to be rid of all that responsibility.

Asking the Right Questions

Now let's get back to our muscle-bound friend. First, Samson was hanging out in the wrong places. Second, he chose the wrong person for the wrong reason. Third, he went back home and told his parents, (yes, *told* his parents, which indicates that something else was very wrong) to get this young Philistine woman for him because "she is all right in my eyes."

Hello? Since when has this been reliable criteria? I think the last time I read my Bible, it said: "Can two walk together, unless they are agreed?" (Amos 3:3). What about simple background material: "So, where are you from?" "Tell me about your family." "What do you like to do in your spare time?" You know, the familiar litany you nurse and rehearse on every first date. It's an exercise of which many of us have grown weary but, nevertheless, it's extremely necessary.

And, when you ask those questions, please, please, puh-leeze! listen carefully to the answers! They can be very revealing. Also find out how he relates to his mother and his sisters because that's how he is going to relate to you.

It's also a good idea to ask him what his goals and plans are for the future. Does he have a vision for his life? You don't want a man who doesn't (and don't assume it's your job to provide one for him, either). And if he rattles off a list of things that doesn't include a committed relationship or plans to have a family or, worse yet, if he boldly tells you he is not interested in marriage for quite a while, believe him. Move on. Or slip him into the friendship file.

When a man says a serious relationship is not on his immediate agenda, we sometimes imagine we can change his mind. Not so. Men are funny that way. They decide to get married, then they start looking for their mates. Women, on the other hand, fall in love and then decide to get married. Would you get on a highway that was going in the opposite direction of where you wanted to go? Well, don't get involved with a man who will take you in the opposite direction of your heart's desire, either.

A date once told me, while expressing his interest in me, "Well, we're both adults." He meant that we were both old enough not to become upset if things didn't work out. The outcome of the relationship was already inevitable. Or what about this line, "Let's go with the flow, and see what happens." Come on! How would you feel if your stockbroker, or your attorney, or anyone who was in the position of helping you make important decisions in your life said that to you?

Of course, the first thing you should check out is a man's spiritual state. That's a given. If you start sharing about the things of God and he looks as if you're speaking in a foreign language, you're in trouble. Christianity, however, is not the total essence of commonality. Not all Christians get along. Be nosy. Ask questions (although do this in good taste). In case you're a little foggy on your motivation, you are gathering information to see if you have enough in common with this person to consider his advances seriously, should he decide to pursue you. Allow me to repeat: *should he decide to pursue you.*

Last, but certainly not least, check out his friends. If you don't have interests in common with his friends, chances are you don't have much in common with your dream man, and whatever is keeping you two together won't last long.

Partners Not Playmates

Like Samson, men sometimes go after the wrong women. They marry women who are "all right in their eyes," who entice their senses, or promote their image. Many of these men are the ones who end up having affairs with their secretaries or with a close family friend. Their excuses are always the same: "She understands me"; "I can talk to her"; "I needed a friend." Why? Because after the sexual attraction wore off and real life set in, the man realized he needed a life companion who was also his friend. Unfortunately, he figured it out too late.

Remember, God created Eve to be a "helper" for Adam, not a playmate. Although God added some delightful features for their mutual enjoyment, He understood that Adam would need a supportive and loving friend in order to deal with the stresses of life. Do you have any idea how strong a marriage can be when a husband and wife are each other's best friend, when they are truly one? Extremely powerful and solid!

In the beginning, when the whole earth was as one people, of one language, of one accent and mode of expression, God said, "Nothing that they propose to do will be withheld from them" (Genesis 11:6). That's pretty potent. Way back in the beginning of Genesis, Satan knew what the power of being one in a marriage could mean. He didn't like it then, and he doesn't like it now.

Today the lust of the flesh (the craving for sensual gratification), the lust of the eyes (the greedy longings of the heart), and the pride of life (the boasting of all we have and do) cloud the minds of men and women in this most crucial area of their lives—that of choosing a life mate. I believe Satan has particularly attacked men in this area because a woman can have such a strong effect on a man's life. She affects the way he looks, the way he works, his sense of well-being. You name it, she affects it.

The Bible implies that a man's reputation is based on his wife. It says that "a virtuous and worthy wife (earnest and strong in character) is a crowning joy to her husband, but she who makes him ashamed is as rottenness in his bones" (Proverbs 12:4 AMP). Proverbs 31:23 (AMP) tells us, "[The virtuous woman's] husband is known in the city's gates, when he sits among the elders of the land."

No wonder the enemy works overtime to keep the right people apart! When a man's marriage is destroyed, the effect is far-reaching. It stretches beyond the home to the church, to the community, even to the nation. In some cases, the effect is very subtle. For instance, broken homes bear a seemingly unnoticeable but direct effect on the moral fiber of this country. Shattered families have caused an increase in gang membership, which leads to an increase in crime, and on and on the ripple effect goes. And that's just one example. There are hundreds of other consequences that grow out of the same disease.

Bringing the House Down

Back to Samson. The story says that he went "down" and talked with the woman he had chosen, and she pleased Samson.

Now on the way "down" to the woman's house, a lion roared at Samson. He killed it and continued on his way. After a while, Samson returned and "turned aside" to see the carcass of the lion, only to find that there was a swarm of bees and honey in the body of the lion. He then scooped some of the honey into his hands and gave it to his parents.

This was another violation of the law. Samson was not supposed to touch a dead body (it was considered unclean). So now his parents have eaten the honey from the unclean thing. Then the father went "down" to the woman's house, too.

Samson was bringing the whole family "down."

Despite all this going "down" and "turning aside," Samson doesn't seem to have a conscience about his obvious violations of God's laws. Instead of repenting, he capitalizes on the encounter with the lion and turns the whole episode into a riddle for his wedding party guests. If they cannot solve the puzzle, the grand prize is a new wardrobe for Samson. Well, this didn't sit well with the wedding guests at all. They'd already bought new outfits to style and profile at the wedding, and they'd purchased gifts for the bride and groom! The wedding was quickly becoming a more expensive affair than previously budgeted for, and they were not going to take this lying down.

Off they went to confront the blushing bride, demanding to know if she had invited them to her wedding to bring them to poverty. They threatened to burn down her and her father's household if she didn't get Samson to tell her the answer to the riddle. So girlfriend boo-hooed for seven whole days until Samson got tired and told her the answer, which she promptly told her countrymen.

I imagine that Samson was more than a little hot under the collar when they smugly gave him the answer. Visions of a new wardrobe dissipated quickly only to be replaced by something far more dangerous—a murderous temper tantrum that ended with 30 men dead and looted. You see, the other end of the equation was that Samson had to give the 30 guests each a change of clothes. You didn't think he was going to destroy his budget did you? No! He killed 30 Philistines instead.

In the meantime, his bride was given to his best friend. Do I have to tell you what happened when Samson found out? I didn't think so, but I'll tell you anyway. Samson went completely off. He destroyed the crops of the Philistines, which left them hungry—and with a very bad taste in their mouths. They went "down" to the house of Samson's wife and burned her and her fathers' household down. With that mission accomplished, they proceeded to threaten the men of Judah and demanded that they hand over Samson.

Samson, not being one to go down without a fight, pretended to go peacefully until he was face-to-face with his disgruntled fan club. Then the Bible says the spirit of the Lord came upon him, and Samson killed 1,000 men with the jawbone of a donkey! Whew! It must have been a humbling experience because the Bible records that he calmed down after that and judged and defended Israel without any further incident (that we know of) for 20 years until he met Delilah. We'll talk about that situation in a minute.

Seeking Parental Advice

Let's take note of several important points. First, when Samson selected this woman in the face of his parents' disapproval, the Bible states that they did not know that this thing was of the Lord—"that He was seeking an occasion to move against the Philistines" (Judges 14:4). Amazing, isn't it? God can use our lives even when we are not submitted to Him. He used Samson's disobedience to accomplish His own purpose of destroying the Philistines. In His foreknowledge, He recognized Samson's temperament and what the end result of his little adventure would be.

That, however, doesn't mean you should ignore your parents' opinions about the person you submit to them as your future life partner. Prayerfully listen to what they have to say.

They know you, and they will see things about that man that you won't notice while you're basking in the glow of romance.

Furthermore, let's face it—you are still under their spiritual umbrella until you are married. God is using them to guide you whether you like what they are saying or not. If you don't agree with them, pray and wait. This little saying sums it up:

> When the situation is wrong and you are wrong,
> God says "no."
>
> When the situation is wrong and you are right,
> God says "slow."
>
> When the situation is right and you are wrong,
> God says "grow."
>
> When the situation is right and you are right,
> God says "go."

Sometimes God uses people like our parents and friends to adjust our timing. At other times He uses them to save us from devastating damage. Oh, to finally reach the place of trusting God enough to believe that His prevention is for our own protection. . . .

Flirting with Temptation

The second note to make here is that God didn't say, "Do not be unequally yoked together with unbelievers" just to give you fewer men from which to choose and to make your life miserable. He said it because he knows that the weaker person will almost always drag the stronger one down. You can rationalize until you are blue in the face that you will lead that man to the Lord and show him everything he needs to know. The truth of the matter is that you probably will fall "down" somewhere along the way while trying.

Picture two oxen yoked together. What happens when the weaker ox can't keep up with the stronger one? The stronger one steps back to accommodate the slower pace of the weaker one. The same with us. We might not start off with that plan in mind, we might not do it on purpose, but we are only human.

Most of us don't plan to sin, but any time we flirt with temptation long enough to fall into the water, we can never say it was an accident. We always get wet when we refuse to move, even when we see the wave coming. Second Timothy 2:22 says, "Flee also youthly lusts." It's childish to take chances in order to win love, to gain the satisfaction and fulfillment we've been longing for. We tend to make irresponsible and bad choices in the face of what our Father has taught us. That's what children do.

The Bible is clear that those who want to languish in immorality and disobedience to God will not see the kingdom of God. I believe God intended for us to enjoy the benefits of kingdom living even while we're here on earth. The kingdom of God is truly "righteousness [right standing with God] and peace [peace with God, yourself, and others] and joy in the Holy Spirit [the kind of joy that surpasses worldly happiness, that goes deep down, past surface happiness]" (Romans 14:17). That means the kingdom of God is more than a physical place. It is a place inside you that *you can enjoy now.*

Samson and Delilah

In case you're thinking Samson learned his lesson about women, you must have forgotten about Delilah. What a knucklehead Samson was! He didn't learn a thing! Off he went with another Philistine woman, so ruled by lust for her that he fell prey to the same mistakes again. This time it cost him more than just a wife. It cost him his life.

> Some time later, [Samson] fell in love with a woman in the Valley of Sorek whose name was Delilah. The rulers of the Philistines went to her and said, "See if you can lure him into showing you the secret of his great strength and how we can overpower

him so we may tie him up and subdue him. Each one of us will give you eleven hundred shekels of silver."

So Delilah said to Samson, "Tell me the secret of your great strength and how you can be tied up and subdued" (Judges 16:4-6 NIV).

Three times Delilah asked and three times Samson answered. Each time, Delilah found out the lie because the Philistines she called to capture him didn't succeed. However the fourth time Samson was weary with the question, and gave a truthful answer.

You'd think it would be obvious if someone violated your trust three times that they were not in your corner. So what could possibly have made Samson finally tell Delilah the secret of his strength? I think he had a false sense of security. After all, he had gotten away with being in sin and bouncing back strong all the times before. The following sad ending stands as a warning to all of us who are tempted to push the envelope to the utmost degree, wondering how many times we can get away with it.

The story goes that Samson got up as the Philistines descended upon him. He said, "I will go out as I have time after time and shake myself free. For Samson did not know that the Lord had departed from him" (Judges 16:20,21 AMP).

On that note, the Philistines captured him, punched out his eyes, and made him a slave.

There is no such thing as living for the moment. You can lose something in a moment that cannot be recovered in a lifetime. Whatever you thought you were getting away with in private has already been an open scandal in heaven. How can you forget that God is always watching? The Word tells us, "Be sure your sin will find you out" (Numbers 32:23). Some life-altering tragedies are spawned from purely innocent mistakes, but that is not what we're addressing here. I am talking about situations where we should know better, and when we need to be honest with ourselves. That little stolen moment, that little secret sin, can destroy our tomorrows on a permanent basis. It can rearrange our lives in a way we haven't planned on or budgeted for.

And it doesn't stop there. Think of the lives around us that can be affected. The result of our little dalliances and excursions into this-is-what-I-want-for-now land can never be predicted. No one plans to get a broken heart, to die in an automobile accident after a night of partying, or to get AIDS, but it happens. Sometimes it happens in genuine innocence, but more often than we care to admit, tragedies like that spring from deliberate defiance.

How did the tragedies of Samson play out? One day Samson's tormentors were about to totally degrade him, using him as an amusement in a stadium. By then he had quietly regained enough strength to pull down the entire building, crushing everyone inside, including himself. More Philistines were killed that day than he had killed in his entire lifetime. Samson may have had the last word, but talk about sabotaging your love life!

Restored to Love, Again

God does not want to keep making sweet potato pie out of our messy lives. Some might say, "Well, at least he was able to make pie out of it," but think how much sweeter the pie would be minus the sour ingredients of residual consequences. If marriage truly is your goal, start being honest with yourself today. Take a look at those repetitious patterns, figure out what your role is in making them happen, repent, and break out of it. Remember, the truth is what sets us free!

And don't give up on yourself. After all of Samson's mistakes he is still listed in the book of Hebrews' "hall of faith" with the mighty people of God. So don't allow the enemy to make you think your mistakes are unredeemable and that you've missed your opportunities. God knew when you would finally get it, and He saved that special man for such a time as this. No time has been wasted in God's perfect design for your life—He simply allowed you to kill a couple of Philistines along the way.

Fortunately, you can be wiser than Samson and not end up anni-
hilating yourself in the temple of repeated mistakes. You can
say:

> *I am free*
> > *free to love as never before*
> > > *throwing open*
> > > > *windows and doors*
> > > > > *rejoicing in my wholeness*
> > > > > *I see clearly*
> > > > *as I run with purpose*
> > > *choosing the right road*
> > > *no longer stumbling*
> > > > *over my own neediness*
> > > > > > *I move*
> > > > > *even paced*
> > > > *head high*
> > > > *shoulders back*
> > > *heart firmly in place*
> > > *making choices with my head*
> > > > *not from my heart*
> > > *ignoring the demands of the flesh*
> > > > *I stretch my spirit*
> > > > > *and respond to God's voice*
> > > > *running eagerly*
> > > > > *toward His instruction*
> > > > *caught up in His potent promises*
> > > *I am bound to Him*
> > > > *a willing love slave*
> > > > > *yet freer than I've ever been*
> > *finding the lost pieces of myself*
> > > *I foolishly gave to others*
> > *casting pearls before the swine*
> > > *once weeping*
> > > > *over the trampled pieces of my heart*
> > > *I am now restored to give again*
> > > > *to one more deserving . . .*

I discover I am
  lost in Him
    only to be found in the truth
      stronger than ever
        ready to love better
      because now I have more to give
  and I will give
    carefully
    abundantly
      and only at His leading
  and in that understanding
    I rest
      I fly
        I am free!

11
Looking in the Mirror

❦

We've spent some time exploring how to get our inner selves together. Now let's take a look at the outside. Believe me, no matter how spiritual your dream man may be, the outside package will still be an important issue. A significant part of a man's makeup centers around the fact that he is moved by what he sees.

Spiritual + Beautiful = Desirable

Sometimes when a woman feels she has been waiting a bit too long, the willingness to fight the good fight of personal upkeep suffers. A lot of women have a hard time being self-motivated to look their best unless a man is on the horizon. Don't get caught making the same observation as the Shulamite woman in Song of Songs, who said, "My own vineyard I have not kept." A lady-in-waiting should always look the part whether a knight is in sight or not. After all, you never know when he'll appear. And when he does, spiritual plus beautiful equals highly desirable.

I cannot tell you how many times I've heard: "I don't know why Christian men like to go out with worldly women when there's a whole church full of women just waiting for a good, saved man to come along." I'll tell you one reason: Women in the world are keenly aware that if you want to catch a fish, you've got to have the right bait. Perhaps they overdo it a bit, but that's because without God they are their only source, so they work a little harder to get what they want. They put a lot of energy into looking good and making themselves appealing to the opposite sex.

Christian women, on the other hand, know their ultimate source is the King. However, having the Lord as your source for all things does not mean you should shirk your personal responsibilities. Don't make His job any harder than it already is!

I have watched a subtle deception weave its way through the church. Many attractive men and women come to the Lord and, overnight, they look like different people. And I'm not talking about a change for the better. The women turn plain, the men look strange and dowdy. I've scratched my head many times and wondered what happened. Then I remembered that I, too, went through this stage of "conversion." I recall being told that my appearance and holiness could not co-exist peacefully, and that if I were truly "saved" I should look saved. At the time, I never stopped to ask, "What do saved people look like?"

I was anxious to please God and convince those around me that I had experienced a life-changing encounter with my Savior. Since I didn't have enough knowledge of the Word to know what was important to God, I fell victim to the legalistic opinions of people around me. I went from one extreme to the other: from a ton of makeup to no makeup, from skin-tight clothes to anything that resembled a tent. It was ridiculous. I thank God that as I began to acquire a deeper understanding of His Word and started to meet other mature Christians, I gained a wonderful thing called balance.

Did God really intend for Christian men and women to walk around devoid of physical appeal? I think not. I think that Satan would like us to believe this subtle lie cleverly wrapped under the guise of "true" holiness. That way believers would never be attracted to one another. After all, "a house divided against itself will not stand" (Matthew 12:25).

The Bible has far too many stories relating how beautiful the women were and how handsome the men were for me to believe that God dismisses the importance of our appearance. And after you've exhausted yourself with being "spiritual," you too will admit that looks are important. Tell the truth: Have you prayed and asked the Lord to send you an unattractive man? No, I didn't think so.

Three Levels of Beauty

So let's talk about beauty, sex appeal, whatever you want to call it. True beauty operates on three levels—soul, mind, and body. When all three are in effect, the results can be astounding. When one is off, it can throw the whole ball game. Have you ever met a man who was physically a work of art, but you had a hard time seeing his attractiveness because his personality stunk? The same holds true for women.

The world has made being beautiful even harder by raising the standard to unrealistic proportions. How many of us will ever be a perfect size 8, be 36-26-36, and never have a gray hair or bump on our face? One famous talk show host shared with the world that she hired a live-in cook, a personal trainer, and worked out twice a day everyday to achieve her svelte body. But how many of us have the money or the time for that?

As Paul says, "All things are lawful for me, but all things are not helpful. All things are lawful for me, but I will not be brought under the power of any" (1 Corinthians 6:12). It's easy to be brought under the power of the world's idea of beauty, but, if you buy into it, one of two things will occur: You either will become obsessed with achieving it or you will drown in the sea of low self-esteem.

As we've noted before, God says we are not to be "conformed to this world, but be transformed by the renewing of your mind, that you may prove what is that good and acceptable and perfect will of God" (Romans 12:2). I believe there is a good, acceptable, and perfect will of God concerning beauty. And the first thing that makes us beautiful is righteousness (holiness).

A man is looking for a woman he can trust. In his world, where competition abounds, he needs to know that one thing is safe—his heart. He feels confident that he can defend everything else. The husband of the virtuous woman "trusts in her confidently and relies on and believes in her securely" (Proverbs 31:11 AMP).

A woman who controls her passions and walks with a sensitive conscience before the Lord is attractive to a man. In a world where women have become more liberal, uninhibited, and overtly aggressive than ever before, a truly godly woman is a precious commodity, even to men "in the world." Every man wants a woman he doesn't have to worry about. He has too many other dragons to fight, and he doesn't need a woman who will be an unprofitable distraction.

Remember the Bible story in Genesis 12, when Abram and Sarai passed through Egypt on their way to the land that God had promised? Abram decided to say that Sarai was his sister so that the Pharaoh wouldn't kill him in order to have Sarai for himself. Sure enough, the fame of her beauty spread throughout Egypt, and news of it reached the Pharaoh. He took Sarai into his harem to make her his wife, but before he could get to her, God intervened and struck the household with plagues until he gave her back to Abram. That's a pretty extreme example of what the wrong woman can do to a man's kingdom. Sarai was wrong for the Pharaoh, but right for Abram. The wrong woman can be a plague in a man's life and affect every area of his existence and well-being.

The Right Spirit

What else constitutes the kind of beauty that God considers good, acceptable, and perfect? Well, we are instructed by the Word that our "beauty should not come from outward adornment, such as braided hair and the wearing of gold jewelry and fine clothes, instead it should be that of your inner self, the unfading beauty of a gentle and quiet spirit, which is of great worth in God's sight" (1 Peter 3:3,4 NIV). This is the type of woman a man runs toward. There are several Scriptures in the book of Proverbs that give clues as to which type of woman will send him packing in a hurry. As expected, she's the opposite of quiet and gentle—she's quarrelsome and ill-tempered.

Let me point out that a gentle and quiet spirit does not suggest that a woman should never have anything to say. It's an attitude, a lifestyle that nurtures and cares, that knows when to listen, and knows when and how to uplift. A gentle, quiet spirit influences more than it instructs. It guides without words, and communicates more with a look or a touch than words could express in a lifetime. Are you getting the picture?

Sometimes I think the Women's Liberation movement has done more harm than good, especially in the area of relationships. The purpose for which the movement began (equal employment, rights, pay, and so on.) has been lost in the mad dash to flex muscles and jockey for control on all fronts, even in areas where gaining the upper hand proves to be detrimental in the long run. You can take my word for it or find out the hard way: Power plays have no place in romance. In a power struggle, where is the victory when you end up being lonely after you've proven your point?

As we've already seen, manipulation is not the answer either. First, Proverbs 14:22 (NIV) says, "Do not those who plot evil go astray? But those who plan what is good find love and faithfulness." Second, when a man finds out (and he will find out) that he has been manipulated, the sweet taste of perceived victory can turn more bitter than you ever imagined possible. Deception ruptures trust. It makes even the most physically beautiful woman look unattractive to a man.

Learning to Like Yourself

The greatest beauty secret a woman can have is righteousness. The Bible says, "From Zion, perfect in beauty, God shines forth" (Psalm 50:2 NIV). It also warns that "charm is deceptive, and beauty is fleeting; but a woman who fears the LORD is to be praised. Give her the reward she has earned, and let her works bring her praise at the city gate" (Proverbs 31:30 NIV). In other words, you will reap what you sow. If you plant respect, trust, and love in your man's heart—and he's a good man—you will gather an incredible bouquet of commitment, love, provision, and protection. The other side of the coin is too unpleasant to speak of.

I once dated a man who told me, "If I met myself walking down the street, I would want to be my friend." I thought that was a very powerful remark at the time, and I wondered if I felt that way about myself. The truth is, if you don't like yourself, no one else will either. Why should they? "As a man thinketh in his heart so is he" (Proverbs 23:7 KJV). If you think you're unlovable, guess what—you are probably already starting to live up to your "image."

Years ago I had a male friend who would tell me how beautiful I was all the time; however, his compliments only made me angry! I thought he was being insincere and trying to make a move on me. I could not receive the compliment gracefully because every time he told me I was pretty, an old tape would go on in my head telling me things quite to the contrary.

You see, as a child I was definitely an ugly duckling—and no one minded telling me so. By the time I reached adulthood and was transformed into a fairly presentable swan (it's still hard for me to say I'm pretty), the words "I am ugly" were etched in stone in my heart. I felt I had learned how to compensate for my shortcomings, but nothing that merited embracing the silly notion that I was actually "beautiful"!

Little did I know that my thought process was making me "act out" on the surface. I couldn't face the world without being totally "done." If someone caught me without my makeup on and without every hair in place, I would respond like a vampire cornered by sunlight.

Fortunately, God began to deal with me. I noticed that the more comfortable I became with myself, the less fixin' up I thought I needed. I learned to praise God because I was fearfully and wonderfully made. If everything that God made was good, "intricately and curiously wrought (as if embroidered with various colors)" (Psalm 139:15 AMP), who was I to insult Him and say He had done a lousy job when it came to me? Or, as the Word puts it more eloquently, "Woe to [her] who strives with [her] Maker!—a worthless piece of broken pottery among other pieces equally worthless (and yet presuming to strive with [her] Maker)! Shall the clay say to him who fashions it, What do you think you are making? or, Your work has no handles?" (Isaiah 45:9 AMP).

In other words, God made us all the way He determined best, in line with His own superior knowledge and for His purpose. And in His thinking, you and I are fine just the way we are. So cast down those thoughts that exalt themselves against the knowledge of God (as far as God is concerned, you are beautiful!), and bring "into captivity every thought to the obedience of Christ" (2 Corinthians 10:5 KJV). How do we do that? By refocusing.

Think about all your assets. Yes, you have some because God made you. Reflect on your best gifts.

> Whatever things are true, whatever things are noble, whatever things are just, whatever things are pure, whatever things are lovely, whatever things are of good report, if there is any virtue and if there is anything praiseworthy—meditate on these things" (Philippians 4:8).

This can present a challenge because Satan loves to invite himself for tea, bringing you're-ugly-and-no-one-is-ever-going-to-love-you pies. Follow that with a sip of why-would-anybody-ever-want-me tea, and you're finished. You're out of the ball game before the anthem has been sung.

Before long, you begin to carry yourself that way. You avoid eye contact, you slouch over, you look a little discolored around the edges. The spirit of rejection walks in front of you shooing away all possible candidates for your hand. Worse yet, you sabotage every relationship—it's called "I'll get you before you get me." But the only person who really gets got is you. So out with the lies, in with the truth.

The Love Factor

The truth is that Jesus loves you. As a matter of fact, you love Him because He first loved you, according to 1 John 4:19. Now that might not seem so comforting if the desire of your heart is a physical love, but follow my line of reasoning. Have you ever noticed that people who already have someone tend to attract even more suitors? It's because they radiate self-satisfaction. It's very appealing. When a woman knows she is loved, her whole countenance radiates a state of well-being, which draws others to her. Both men and women want whatever she has. So, if you really allow yourself to feel the love that Jesus has for you and learn how to enjoy it, the same effect will be achieved.

And check this out: The love Jesus has for you is deep! He says that nothing can separate you from His love, not "death nor life, neither angels nor demons, neither the present nor the future, nor any powers, neither height nor depth, nor anything else in all creation will be able to separate us from the love of God that is in Christ Jesus our Lord" (Romans 8:38 NIV). Talk about a tall love, a strong love!

If some man like Antonio Banderas, Brad Pitt, or Denzel Washington (now you know who I like) offered that kind of love to some woman in a movie, we would be beside ourselves with envy. So why don't we react the same way when Jesus tells us that He loves us like that?

The truth is that *you are loved*—so much so, that a man was willing to die for you. So pull those shoulders up, get a smile on that face, add pep to your step, and start behaving like a woman who is loved. This is a major beauty secret: Women who are in love and feel loved have a glow that no store-bought beauty mist can create. They are radiant and very attractive to even the most nonchalant male.

Seeing It Like It Is

Take an honest assessment of your reflection in the mirror. Not perfect, right? But workable. Hey, guess what, no one is perfect! Isn't that liberating? I like to say that God is fair. To one he gave a fabulous body but okay hair. To another he gave fabulous hair but huge feet. Kind of like the spiritual gifts, everyone has something in the plus column. What a sense of humor! I think our good points along with our bad points were designed to keep us all humble.

The last person God created perfect in beauty became so vain he thought that he should be God and started a whole lot of trouble—that's right, Satan himself. So even our beauty deficits are a loving favor from God. And for every deficit there is a way to make it an asset.

Beauty tricks abound in today's society. All sorts of compensations for beauty concerns can be made with a simple brush stroke, additional hair, or wise wardrobe choices. I'm not an advocate of plastic surgery unless you have a really severe disfigurement that cannot be fixed with makeup, a diet, exercise, or the correct clothing. For the most part, our beauty problems are usually greater in our minds than in the eyes of others—and we need to know the difference.

A Natural Beauty

My biggest caution is that whatever you choose to do to enhance your beauty, the operative word should be "natural." If you are inclined to go the hair extension or hair weave route, make sure it looks realistic. Get it cut into a style that is believable. Remember, a woman's hair is her glory, but it shouldn't outdo the rest of who you are.

If the eyes are truly the windows to the soul, you don't want your prospective suitor to be distracted by your makeup. Most men hate makeup, so the less they see, the better. Besides, makeup is to *enhance* your features, not to be a mask. Take advantage of makeup artists. They are at every makeup counter in larger stores ready to give you a makeover for free. So experiment, have fun, and learn.

If you find yourself really piling on the makeup to hide a serious skin problem, chances are you need a good dermatologist or an adjustment in your diet. Skin can be affected by many things, such as reactions to specific foods, vitamin deficiencies, stress, or heredity. Don't let the cost of an office visit scare you away from making an appointment with a specialist who could change your life. Add up how much you are spending on makeup to cover up the problem, and you'll probably decide you really can afford to go after all.

Women in the Bible had a more holistic, natural approach to beauty. They utilized herbs and oils long before they got to makeup. (Remember Esther's 12-month beautification rites?) They knew the importance of having healthy, beautiful skin. This was the secret of maintaining a youthful appearance for many years, and it is an art that seems to be making a comeback. More makeup companies are beginning to realize the healing benefits of botanical properties and are including them in their makeup lines. There are endless possibilities.

The "Body Beautiful"

Now for the part of the honest assessment that's everybody's favorite. Our bodies. Be honest with yourself. Are your expectations realistic? If you've never in your life been a size five, it's probably not a good idea to make this a goal. What are you willing to do to be in shape? Find alternatives you can live with and remain consistent. If you don't like to exercise, walking is a wonderful substitute. I went down two dress sizes by walking for 40 minutes to an hour every morning before I started my day.

I suggest you make your goal to be physically fit (as opposed to being pencil thin). Some men like "a little meat on their bones" as the old folks say, so don't think there is only one body type men find attractive. Ask yourself the bigger question: What do you think of yourself? Do you like the skin you're in or does there need to be a little less of it? If you decide on the latter, make realistic decisions on how to reach your goal.

Crash diets are a no-no. They just mean more pounds later. I highly recommend Weight Watchers as the best diet program. They offer sound instruction that you can follow for the rest of your life. You won't feel deprived, and you'll learn how to eat properly. Another wonderful dietary guide is the Bible. God has quite a few things to say about eating that scientists are beginning to reiterate today.

Perhaps your size is okay but your proportions are where you have a struggle. Way too little of this, a bit too much of that? You'd be amazed how the right cut of clothing can rearrange your silhouette. Again, this is another area where honest advice from salespeople or friends with good taste can prove priceless.

I always felt overweight. To compensate I would dress in loose garments, thinking I was doing a good job of hiding everything. One day a seamstress friend of mine suggested that I should wear more fitted clothing because I had such a small waist. She said it would make me look 20 pounds lighter. As it turned out, she was right. Others noticed the difference immediately and thought I had been dieting. I hadn't done anything except change the way I dressed! What a revelation. And it was painless.

Be straight with yourself and get others you trust to give you an honest appraisal. You might have to let go of some old habits that you thought were cute. You might feel a little shaky at first, but if you tough it out long enough to gauge the reactions around you, you'll be surprised at how quickly you will grow comfortable with those changes. Being honest with yourself definitely has its beauty advantages.

Fast Living, Fast Aging

Another point: Sin is an enemy to beauty. I'm sure you've seen people who look hard, and said to yourself, "Boy, that person has been around the block a few times!" That's what sinful living will get you. Hard features, bad skin, premature wrinkles.

Purity has gotten a bad rap. It's considered by many to be a boring lifestyle, but I see nothing boring about having a clean conscience, and a healthy mind and body. Take a look around you at the ravages of sexual promiscuity, alcoholism, nicotine addiction, and drug abuse. The results speak for themselves. They leave marks on the soul, as well as the outward appearance of a person.

This might sound a little worldly (but too bad 'cause it's true), but men have this strange thing called a "virgin complex." They want a woman who has been, in their eyes, unspoiled. They want to feel that no one else can have what belongs to them. They want a woman who is a lady. They'll play with women who are willing playmates, but they usually marry a completely different type of woman.

Rick James summed it up rather well in a song he wrote back in the seventies. I believe the lyrics went something like this: "She's a freaky kind of girl, the kind you don't take home to mother." He went on to say what a good time he had with her, but when it came down to being serious, he was looking for someone else. So much for beauty that is not pure. On the other hand, references to the "beauty of holiness" are numerous in the Bible. For instance, "a virtuous woman is a crown to her husband" (Proverbs 12:4 KJV).

The Power of Words

Thinking on things that are lovely, lovable, and of good report can dramatically affect the impression you make. It's true that what comes out of the mouth defiles a woman. It is not a lovely thing to listen to a woman speaking bitterly or who is deeply engrossed in gossip. But everyone loves a person who has encouraging or uplifting things to say.

I am not suggesting that you become your man's teacher, because, as you know, he should be the spiritual head of the household. But I encourage you to always have a positive word, and to offer perspectives that are rooted in Christ. These are the things that will build your mate up because "man shall not live by bread alone, but by every word that proceeds from the mouth of God" (Matthew 4:4).

We should be prepared to speak in skillful and godly wisdom. How do we do this? By studying the Word and knowing the mind and heart of your First Love, God Himself. Having a strong foundation of intimacy with Him can only improve the state of your relationship with the physical manifestation of His love (your mate). One friend told me that when she was having her quiet time with the Lord regularly and their relationship was wonderful, her relationship with her husband was incredible. When her relationship with the Lord was dry, her relationship with her spouse was worse than dry. That's good food for thought, isn't it?

Remember—a man falls in love with a woman based on how he feels when he is with her, so words can be very potent. A woman who is an oasis for her man is a lovely creature. In the Song of Songs, the king says "Let me hear your voice; for your voice is sweet and your countenance is lovely." And the Shulamite woman says of him, "His mouth is most sweet, yes, he is altogether lovely."

A man will race home to a woman he knows will have good news or words of encouragement. Words that disquiet his soul or disturb his countenance on a continual basis will drive him away—to workaholism or to find a reason for spending his time away from home, away from her. The sound of your voice and the things you say are more important than you know. Managed in a positive way, this area of your life can be a big beauty bonus for you.

Pretty Is As Pretty Does

According to the Amplified Bible, Philippians 4:8 says, "If there is any virtue and excellence, if there is anything worthy of praise, think on and weigh and take account of these things (fix your mind on them)." So, take note of your best features and accentuate the positive. Work with what you've got, girl-friend, and play it to the hilt. But don't rest your beauty and honor on your physical appearance alone.

Many a gorgeous man has been spotted with a so-so looking woman. If you were to investigate why that man was so happy to have that woman hanging on his arm, you would get an earful about how wonderful she is. In his eyes she is beautiful enough to rival the most famous sex symbol. Through the eyes of love, everything looks beautiful. As 1 Peter 4:8 states, "Love covers over a multitude of sins," including physical shortcomings. Do you want to be the most beautiful woman in your man's world? Start from the inside out.

"Pretty is
as pretty does"
mama used to say . . .
and still
my ears ring
with the gentle warning
as I paint my lips
Marrakech red
dot my cheekbones
with my favorite cashmere blush
gently smudging my eyelids
charcoal gray
enjoying the feel of silk
as my dress glides down
coffee-colored hips
swinging around my ankles
causing me to walk to its rhythm
catching my reflection in the mirror
"shoot, I look good"

But "pretty is
as pretty does"
the thought sobers me

as I wait for the doorbell to ring
knowing I can't rely on my dress
or putting my best face forward
I quiet my spirit
and meditate on what is real
what won't pass away
what will endure
past premature gray
and wrinkles
and all that a woman fears . . .
a quiet and gentle spirit
but can that truly be enough?
I check my reflection
and different eyes
stare back at me
more wise
no longer admiring my artistry
they challenge me
to let them look deeper
beneath the surface
where true beauty lies . . .
the doorbell
interrupts my reverie
I start toward the door
hips swaying softly
perfumed hands reaching for the latch
and I find myself confronted
by roses and a smile
"my, how beautiful you look"
it sounds melodious in my ears
"thank you"
I respond demurely
behind dropped lashes
drinking in the smell of the roses
I find myself
delighting more in their fragrance
than in their color . . .

"*Pretty is as pretty does*"
the roses remind me
as I take his hand
and step into the night
I smile
and breathe a prayer
"*Lord, cover me*
in your loveliness" . . .

In the book of Esther, there is a sad tale. King Ahasuerus (Xerxes) was having a banquet. He decided to call his wife Vashti from her quarters so that his guests could gaze on her beauty. Ahasuerus was extremely proud of her.

The queen refused to come, thus disgracing the king. Upon obtaining counsel, he concluded that her behavior would encourage the other women of the kingdom to be disrespectful to their men.

She was dethroned.

So much for beauty, huh? Now there are several different schools of thought about why Queen Vashti didn't report for beauty duty, but the bottom line is still the same. One minute her beauty was proclaimed, the next she was defamed. It didn't matter how breathtaking she was, her actions were considered ugly and a threat to the balance of authority in every household in the kingdom.

What you do, what you say, what you think—these will always have more impact and a greater lasting impression than your reflection in the looking glass.

Don't just look beautiful, *be* beautiful.

12
Costly Expectations

We've addressed many of the beauty essentials most women think are important to a man. Now, let's talk about some of his expectations. We know, by now that we should beautify ourselves both spiritually and personally but what about our physical environment—our housekeeping habits? Uh-oh, did I hear a collective groan?

Housekeeping for Keeps

The Lord said, through Paul, that it is necessary for older women to teach younger women "to be sober, to love their husbands, to love their children, to be discreet, chaste, keepers at home, good, obedient to their own husbands, so that the word of God be not blasphemed" (Titus 2:4,5 KJV). In Proverbs 31, God chooses to enlighten us on what is considered a wife of noble character. A few key phrases about homemaking caught my eye here as well. Check this out. She "works with eager hands. She is like the merchant ships, bringing her food from afar. She gets up while it is still dark; she provides food for her family. . . . She sets about her work vigorously; her arms are strong for her tasks. She sees that her trading is profitable. . . . She opens her arms to the poor. . . . She has no fear for her household; for all of them are clothed in scarlet. She watches over the affairs of her household and does not eat the bread of idleness" (verses 14-27).

All these things make this woman attractive.

"This is beginning to sound like too much work to me," you may be thinking. If so, let me encourage you to develop good housekeeping habits for yourself, not just to please a man. It is said that it takes 21 days to form a habit, but I think it takes longer than that to become a good housekeeper. Why not start today?

If you are messy in your single life, and then decide to become Susie Homemaker after you march down the aisle, you will be most unhappy shortly after the honeymoon. First, you will blame your husband for all your new tasks and, somehow, you'll make him pay. Second, you will become too overwhelmed to know where to begin. The housework will build up, your new lease on wedded bliss will be short lived, leaving you to face a very irritated spouse. Either way, whether you succeed or not, someone in your home is going to be resentful, and this will cause tension. It is quite difficult to make major changes overnight and expect them to last.

Housekeeping and cooking are two areas where a man may expect or want you to be like his mother. (I'm making a general statement here, which is more often true than not.) He probably got used to his mom picking up after him, making sure he had clean clothes, and providing wonderful home-cooked meals long before you came along. And guess what? You will inherit the role of satisfying those basic expectations. If you fight this, it will become a bone of contention throughout your marriage—if you get to the altar at all. A man loves good food and a clean house. It adds to his sense of security.

Cleanliness and Godliness

Do yourself a favor, begin developing good housekeeping habits now. Do it for your own personal reward. You'll be amazed at the feelings of accomplishment and personal pride you'll experience when you put your house in order. Develop a system that is comfortable for you so housecleaning doesn't become a much-dreaded chore. If you can afford a cleaning woman, by all means don't be ashamed to get one. Whatever it takes, develop the habit of cleanliness. Set chore goals that can realistically be achieved. Perhaps a room a day won't make cleaning so burdensome. Whatever you decide is best for you, do it.

I believe the old adage "cleanliness is next to godliness" is true. Years ago, when I was in school (I won't tell you how long ago that was), as I was leaving my dorm room, I turned back toward the room and gazed at it before I closed the door. It was a mess; things were strewn everywhere. The Lord spoke to me and said, "This room reflects your spiritual condition." That statement scared me half to death! You should have seen me cleaning and sorting when I returned from class.

Over the years, I have noticed a direct correlation between my spiritual condition and my physical surroundings. The more disarray I tolerate, the more lax I am spiritually. When all is tight between me and my Savior, I demand that everything be in order around me. Interesting, wouldn't you say?

Proverbs says that the virtuous woman's arms are strong for her tasks. Strength comes from regular and continuous use. And regularity, at some point, shifts into automatic pilot. If you develop simple habits, such as not leaving dirty dishes in the sink, cleaning out the bathtub and sink before bed, or putting things back in their proper place when you're finished with them, these actions will be business as usual when you're living with another person. (It's the little things that, if neglected, pile up into a big mess.)

Good Cookin'—Good Lovin'

And now for my favorite subject—food! It's one of most men's favorite subjects, too. I recommend that you stock up on some cookbooks, start watching Julia Child, or follow your favorite cook around the kitchen 'cause, honeychile, oh the difference a meal can make!

If the family of the virtuous woman thought she was like a merchant ship bringing food from afar, she must have been jammin' in the kitchen. You know how good food tastes when you're ravenous? It sounds like her food tasted like that all the time. I don't know how large a repertoire she had in the kitchen, but here's my suggestion: Learn how to cook *something!* Accumulate a small list of meals you cook well and gradually add to your list.

I used to have a boyfriend who was always bringing his friends over for my pot roast and potatoes. He was so proud of those potatoes that it was almost comical. He said I was the only woman he knew who could make mashed potatoes taste like soufflé. So you know what I did? I cooked those mashed potatoes a lot. He was hooked. (In case you're wondering what happened, we were going to marry, but, sadly, he went home to be with the Lord. And he never got to sample all of the other wonderful things I learned how to cook.)

I'm telling you, food is important. If hunger made a man sell his birthright (see the story of Esau in Genesis), what do you think? There's nothing like the thought of a wonderful meal to make a man hurry home. It's that oasis effect. The more of an oasis you can create, the more your man will enjoy spending time close to home, close to you. Begin now to form habits that will make your nest the kind of place he wants to hurry to.

What Have You Done for Me Lately?

What do you expect from the man in your life? He's not the only one who should gain from the relationship, you know. Partners should consider what they have to offer and what they stand to gain from a relationship—in that order. Christ laid down His life in order to gain us. This doesn't mean that you spill out all of those wonderful gifts in one overwhelming gush, nor does it mean you dole out generous heaps of wonderfulness on those who are not deserving. Janet Jackson sang a song several years back called "What Have You Done for Me Lately?" I think a little more of this song's attitude needs to be adopted, but with careful balance.

God has decreed a list of responsibilities for men. They are responsible for their women spiritually and physically, to the point of being willing to lay down their lives! Once married, they are to care for their wives as if they were taking care of themselves. That means they should provide food and clothes, and take every precaution necessary to make sure she lives a safe and secure existence. But women's expectations, in light of present-day desperation, have been lowered and compromised.

Prospective husbands no longer have to court women, wine and dine them, or behave like gentlemen. Why? Because too many women are willing to fill in the blanks in the relationship themselves in order to have a man, all in the name of validation. It is a pathetic state of affairs. And yet many of these women still end up unfulfilled or repeatedly alone. I've heard this from the horse's mouth, so to speak. Several of my male friends have made it known to me that they find women who are too eager very unattractive. Remember, nothing won easily is appreciated for very long. When we have to pay a dear price for something or someone, we treasure it always.

Making a Wish List

I would like to encourage you to do a little exercise. Write down the type of man you're looking for. Include, for instance, all of his qualities, and the way you would like to be treated. Write down on a separate list what your needs are in a relationship. I am speaking of realistic expectations such as considerate, communicative, has a vision for his life, has an open conscience toward God. I'm not saying he has to be rich, super-duper fine, knows the whole Bible by heart, movie-type romantic, or generous to breathtaking proportions (although that wouldn't be bad). Friendship and romance should be combined, because your mate should be your best friend. If you are in a relationship presently, check to see how many of the things on your list reflect your present situation. If not, why not?

Ask yourself why you gave up the things on that list. If your response is "I was afraid I'd be alone forever," consider this: Something is not always better than nothing. In most cases, nothing offers more peace of mind and fewer battle scars.

By the way, while you're being realistic, also be fair. Don't expect any more from your boyfriend than what you are willing to be yourself. If you want love and compassion, be a good listener and a blessing yourself. If you want a man with an Arnold Schwartzenegger body, then Jane Fonda's exercise video should be your best friend. If you don't want a man who is in debt, get your own financial house in order. Remember, in most cases you get what you give, and you attract what you are.

Okay, so everybody doesn't have someone in their lives at the present time. Still, make your list. "Write the vision and make it plain . . . for the vision is yet for an appointed time. . . . It will not lie. Though it tarries, wait for it; because it will surely come, it will not tarry" (Habakkuk 2:2,3). If you think some of your expectations are a bit lofty, thus endangering your discernment with the menfolk, ask a wise, married friend to take a look at your list and tell you what is realistic. (Sometimes single women become very codependent on one another, and selfish motives might color their advice. In some cases, your friends might not be as happy about you having a relationship as they say they are or as much as you think. They subconsciously might want you to remain single with them. Your married friends, however, have nothing to lose. And wouldn't you rather get advice from someone who has been successful at building a relationship with a man?)

Don't compromise the important things on your list. After you've spent time grooming yourself to be a gift, make sure he is a good gift, too. Would you get on a plane if you knew the pilot was not qualified to fly? Then why would you consider marrying someone who is not qualified to be a husband? He certainly will not feel the need to change after you marry him—you've already given your stamp of approval "as is." A woman who knows what she wants and what she deserves, and won't settle for less is considered a prize catch by the male species—she's extremely beautiful and very desirable.

You need to know what you deserve so you can have what you deserve. If your self-esteem isn't quite up to snuff, causing you to hem and haw about what you deserve, throw your opinion out of the window and remember what God says a woman deserves: Men who will be responsible for a woman spiritually and physically, who will lay down their lives for their wives, who will provide food, clothing, and safety. Review these attributes until they get down in your spirit and ring in your ears and your heart. You deserve to be nurtured, provided for, and loved. If you find yourself feeling like a stepchild in your relationship with a man, let go and let God bring you a man who knows what time it is. Don't settle—that's what women in the world do, not the King's daughters who reside in their Father's court.

Giving Too Much

The King's daughters needn't give too much too soon, a lifestyle that invariably proves to be detrimental. This concept takes a little longer to master, but it's crucial. Respect and trust have to be earned, so don't throw your best treasures at a man too quickly. Do not assume a role that you haven't been given. In other words, don't do the things a wife does until you are a wife. Be a friend until he carries you over the threshold.

Remember the Scripture that says, "Do not exalt yourself in the king's presence, and do not claim a place among great men; it is better for him to say to you, 'Come up here,' than for him to humiliate you before a nobleman" (Proverbs 25:6,7 NIV). The humiliation of rejection after you've poured out your heart and soul to a person can be devastating. In the eyes of most men, they believe that if they had to fight hard to win you, that means you won't be an easy catch for any other man.

Also, as I've mentioned before, something in their nature demands that they pursue and win their mates. This does not suggest that you should be difficult, but it implies that you should not be easy. Jacob didn't mind working for 14 years to have Rachel as his wife. Wouldn't you like a mate that had that attitude about you (minus the long wait!)? I would.

Finding the Real You

One last point: Be a whole person so that desperation doesn't have a chance to set in. It's a mistake to decide you'll get married first, and *then* find out what God wants you to do with the rest of your life. "Seek first the kingdom of God and His righteousness, and all these things shall be added to you." That's not about God being selfish; it's in your best interest to seek His will. If you are waiting for a husband before you get on with the rest of your life, forget it. You won't meet your man until you get busy. Start pursuing some of those other dreams of yours, the wonderful things that God has put in your heart.

I had a boss once who believed that if a woman gained weight after a man married her, it was grounds for a divorce based on deception. She was no longer the woman he had married. Although he was a little extreme, his point is well taken in concept. Suppose you met a man while you were living a rather sedate life: working nine to five, going to church, spending most evenings at home. He decides you suit his lifestyle perfectly—he's been looking for a woman who lives a simple life. You get married. All of a sudden you decide you want to go to seminary, you want to become a missionary, and you want to travel around the world! Well, what's the poor man to do? He now has a whole lot more on his hands than he bargained for. He is not interested in doing any of those things. He feels guilty, but not enough to catch the vision. You feel trapped by the marriage; you resent him for throwing a monkey wrench into your dreams. This is a major problem.

Just think, if you could have gotten busy living those dreams while you were free, things would have ended up a lot differently. For one thing, he probably wouldn't have gotten involved with you in the first place because he would have known you didn't fit his bill. And that's good news in light of the fact that you probably would have met someone within the circle of your activities who had the same interests as you—someone with whom you could have been equally yoked in the dream department, a perfect partner to complement your life goals.

Your mate is probably waiting on the other side of your dreams. You will meet him when you get on with your life. In the meantime, you will be happy and fulfilled because you will be doing what you were born to do. The wait for your mate won't feel as long, and you won't feel desperate. You will be able to allow the relationship to grow and flow into what it is supposed to be. It is a beautiful thing when two whole people come together to make an even more complete couple. You both bring invaluable gifts to exchange.

Are you sick of waiting? God knows what He is doing, so get real. Get busy. Get whole. Get a life! Because getting involved with a man will not make you any more of a complete person than you already are today.

In Paul's opinion, it is better to remain single. In doing so, men and women are free to give their all in service to God. Paul must have had the gift of singleness. I think he knew that because he went on to say, "but if they cannot exercise self-control, let them marry. For it is better to marry than to burn with passion" (1 Corinthians 7:9).

Although I don't believe I have "the gift," I understand what Paul is saying. There are many things I have experienced in life that would never have happened if I had been married. I love to travel; no way could I go gallivanting off to Africa for a whole month, or to Paris, or to many of the other places I frequently go whenever the mood hits me.

I take advantage of the fact that I am not obligated to anyone but myself and the Lord. I delight in all the exciting opportunities that are set before me. I know there will be a more sober time in life when I will have a husband and children, which will color some of my options. I will no longer be able to be a gypsy, footloose and fancy free. And I won't mind, either, because I have lived a fascinating life. It will just become wonderful in a different way.

It's up to you: If you wait to live until after you're married, you'll find yourself sitting around saying, "If I coulda, woulda, shoulda." Or you can discover the fullness of life God meant for you now, and allow your mate to encounter you while you're actively doing your thing. Let him see exactly what he will be getting—a beautiful, vibrant woman excited about life and the part she's playing in it. This is very attractive to men. Men like to see the women they're interested in feeling fulfilled, being all that they can be. Give him a reason to boast.

I saw her from afar
        enjoying life to the fullest
            moving confidently
                through her dreams
                    weaving new dreams
                        arms open
                        as if expecting
                    more blessings than she could hold
                    and I wanted her . . .
        I wanted to drink from her life
    to taste
what she thought was so sweet
I wanted to fall asleep
        hearing her laughter
            and wake up in her arms
                so strong
                    so warm
                so able to live
                and able to love at the same time . . .
        I wanted to wander through
    the maze of her mind
and discover each fascinating thought
    each unspoken question
        I wanted to know
            who she was . . .

> *every facet*
> > *every flaw*
> > > *every strength*
> > *every weakness . . .*
> *I wanted her to*
> *need me*
> *to not need me*
> *to want me*
> *to not want me*
> *like an elusive butterfly*
> > *drawn to the color*
> > *of my love*
> > > *already drunk*
> > > > *from the honey of the Son*
> > > *while she decides*
> > *whether to alight*
> *and partake or not*
> *I have already decided.*
> *I want her . . .*

So now he wants you, you want him, and the two of you are ready to commit yourselves to a lasting, lifetime relationship. And by this time, you are more able to see the big picture clearly, and to view the upcoming scenery—engagement and marriage—objectively.

Is marriage—not just any marriage, but marriage to that one, specific man in your life—going to offer you a better life than the one you now enjoy? For everything you receive, there will be areas in which you have to give of yourself gladly and, at times, sacrificially. Today is the day to begin taking a realistic look at the requirements of building and maintaining a healthy, vibrant relationship. I'm talking about a love that will continue into marriage and last the rest of your life.

Like most good things, lasting love doesn't happen without work. The following chapters provide some kingdom rules for a successful partnership. Consider them a sort of Lamaze class for marriage. The exercises won't lessen the difficulties, but at least they will prepare you for the labor of love.

Please remember, "No pain, no gain." This succinct, modern-day maxim certainly applies to more than physical exercise. Every successful relationship requires dying to self, and dying to self is difficult. Even though the results ultimately bring more joy, it's a painful process that occurs often as you speak, as you submit, as you seek God's best for your future.

13
Love Talk

Can we talk?
  heart to heart
    soul to soul
      in unspoken whispers
        communing in the spirit
        sharing our pain
      without cutting one another's heart
      exchanging our tears
    without shouting at each other's eyes
    without pointing
    accusatory words
  exchanging justifications
    for unheard sentiments . . .

Can we talk?
  like the friends
    we promised to be
      like the lovers we once were
        hanging
  on each other's every word
    reveling in each other's breath
      we took no easy offense

too eager were we to please
too busy being
on good behavior
we put our
best language forward
speaking in loving caresses
no problem
being too hard to solve
if we put our
heads
and our hearts together
gently
oh so tenderly
touching one another's
bruises and fears
cleansing
and soothing them
with words of comfort
and reassurance
with nothing between us
to offer resistance
we were honest
we were open
speaking the truth
in love
seasoned with grace
we sought
not to offend
but to free one another
to love more
than before . . .
but now we've grown
less careful
numbed by
days grown
too identical and familiar
in each other's presence . . .

> nothing has changed but us
> bumping into one another's feelings
> stepping over each other's spirits
> ignoring each other's souls,
> we talk behind each other's hearts
> until we become
> convenient strangers
> trapped in silent habits
> prisoners of senseless rages
> flailing to find the point
> where we first began
> paralyzed from lack
> of a map
> we sit
> we wait
> we sigh . . .
> we shy
> away
> from the obvious . . .
> can we talk?

I have a confession to make. I have been watching a soap opera lately. Normally, I'm not a TV person, but recently I was injured and spent a bit of time convalescing. I became intrigued with the storyline on one of the soaps because, for me, it became a real character study in how different types of behavior affect love relationships.

More specifically, this little drama helped me identify the various ways people choose to communicate. I am amazed that women throughout the ages have given birth to nations, provoked men to go to war, changed the history of the world, and yet still can't figure out how to communicate effectively with their husbands.

Commune, Communion, Communicate

God appeals to us, "Come now, and let us reason together. . . . Though your sins are like scarlet, they shall be as white as snow; though they are red like crimson, they shall be as wool. If you are willing and obedient, you shall eat the good of the land" (Isaiah 1:18). God calls us to come and reason with Him so He can free us from our sins, free us to enjoy the good of the land. He understands that initially we might not see everything His way, but after He has lovingly explained the error of our ways we'll willingly respond out of the love we have for Him. When we respond to His call to repentance, the barrier between us and God is broken. He gains a new child in the kingdom, and we gain unlimited access to Him and freedom from sin.

In human communication, each person usually has a personal agenda he or she wishes the other person to line up with. It becomes the focal point of the conversation, often without any thought being given to the other person's feelings or wishes. That agenda usually is not presented in a "come let us reason together" manner, which means having a nonjudgmental respect for the other person's position. (We are to "discern" if an action is wrong or right. We are not to "judge" the punishment the person deserves for his or her wrongdoing. That is God's job, and His alone.)

Anger stems from what we view as our violated rights. Impasses in relationships come from failing to recognize the rights of others and failing to respect the other person's feelings. Right or wrong, another person's feelings are very real. The more we ignore that reality, the less progress we make with our own requests.

The most common complaint between men and women who are struggling to communicate with one another is, "He (or she) doesn't understand me!" It may sound trite, but if we are to communicate our needs and our desires effectively, we must understand the meaning and goal of "communication."

Commune, communion, communicate. These words are all born out of one another. If you look in Webster's dictionary, you will be struck as I was by some very interesting definitions.

Some of these meanings hadn't really occurred to me before. I submit some of them for your consideration and meditation.

> To administer or receive Communion; to talk over, to impart, participate, *an act or instance of sharing,* to convey knowledge of or information about, make known, to reveal by clear signs, to cause to pass from one to another, to open into each other: to convey or transmit something intangible, a process by which information is exchanged between individuals through a common system of symbols, signs, or behavior, *intimate fellowship* or personal rapport, *mutual participation.* (Emphasis added.)

When it comes to getting our needs across to the man in our lives, there is no room for opera singing—no time for "me, me, me." I may have needs, but I still have to consider the feelings and needs of the other person. This is why one of the first things counselors usually teach about communication skills is never say "*you* do this" or "*you* make me feel like that." Instead, we are to say, "*I* feel this way when this or that happens." This eliminates accusation. It frees the other person to respond to what you've experienced. It enables him (or her) to know what his (or her) role was in the misunderstanding. Accusation, on the other hand, puts the other person on the defensive, which usually accomplishes nothing or the wrong thing.

Jezebel, Queen of Confrontation

The Bible gives us a glimpse at what being confrontational will get you. An Old Testament Queen, Jezebel, became quite famous for her boldness. Her name has been associated with all the wrong types of feminine behavior throughout history. She was a real "sapphire," a cold, mean, hard woman. She didn't "take no mess," honey. She served it up, but she didn't take it.

When Jezebel's husband, Ahab, got depressed because a peasant named Naboth wouldn't sell him his vineyard, she devised a scheme to have Naboth accused, condemned, and killed. Then she sent Ahab out to take ownership of Naboth's land. This was a woman used to running things. She ran her husband; she ran the prophets of Baal; and she tried, unsuccessfully, to run the prophets of God.

Jezebel was used to having her way most of the time, so the thought that a "soft answer turns away wrath, but a harsh word stirs up anger" never occurred to her. Unfortunately, at a time when she should have exercised a little discretion, she fell into her usual bold behavior.

When Jehu was anointed as king and rode into Jezreel, Jezebel painted her eyes, arranged her hair, looked out of the window, and shouted, "Have you come in peace, you treacherous murderer, you?" (See 2 Kings 9:30-36.)

This didn't make a good impression on the new king, who promptly had her thrown from the tower she was calling from, and his horses trampled her underfoot. By the time the king had gone in, finished eating a meal, and decided to have her laid to rest, the burial party found nothing except her skull, her feet, and her hands. That's what bad communication skills will get you!

Abigail, Daughter of Diplomacy

Let's juxtapose that story with another one about a woman who needed great communication skills in order to procure personal security for herself and her household. Abigail is noted in the Bible not only as a persuasive speaker, but as one who could see beyond herself, assess the big picture, and know where to leave room for God to act on her behalf. In 1 Samuel 25, the story goes that Abigail was married to a rich man named Nabal. While David was on the run, he and his men had been protecting Nabal's work force. When David sent some of his men to ask Nabal for some food, which was a customary courtesy, Nabal told them to get lost. This didn't make David particularly happy. He organized his men to wipe out Nabal and all the males of his household. In the nick of time, one of the servants went to Abigail with a word of warning.

Abigail lost no time. She flew into action, rounding up more-than-generous rations for David's men. Scripture doesn't mention her painting her eyes or arranging her hair, but it does say that she went out to meet David and his men, and that she bowed herself to the ground as he approached her. That's right, she humbled herself. She then went on to apologize for her husband's behavior, owning up to the fact that her husband was like his name—a fool (Nabal means fool).

Abigail explained to David that she knew he was God's anointed, and that it would not be in his best interest to have blood on his hands. She was concerned for his conscience, and reminded him that the Lord would take care of his enemies, that it was not necessary for him to attend to them personally. David was struck by her imploring speech and remarked that she should be blessed for her good judgment. He bade her, "Go up to your house. See, I have heeded your voice and respected your person" (1 Samuel 25:35).

When she arrived home, Nabal was in the middle of hosting a huge banquet. He was in high spirits, very drunk, and none the wiser as to what had taken place. Abigail didn't fuss at him. Instead, she held her peace until morning. When he was sober, she politely told him what had happened.

Well, Nabal had a heart attack and fell into a coma right then and there. Ten days later the Lord struck him, and he died. Here's the added bonus: When David heard about Nabal's death, he sent word to Abigail asking her to become his wife. Because of her graciousness, she ended up married to the king of Israel. Now that's what I call communicating!

Esther, Empress of Finesse

We've already met Queen Esther, but she deserves another visit here, because she was a master communicator. In the book of Esther, we find Haman, who hated the Jews. Why? Because Mordecai, Esther's Jewish uncle, wouldn't bow to him in the gates. Based on this personal slight, Haman devised a way to get the king to exterminate the Jews from all of the provinces in his dominion.

Once Mordecai heard about this, he sent a message to Esther telling her she had to get to the king and do something, because, perhaps, she had attained her royal position for such a time as this! Esther knew very well that she couldn't come up with a way to intervene on her own; she needed divine intervention. She requested that everyone fast and pray for three days and nights.

On the third day, Esther put on her royal robes, beautified herself, and went and stood in the inner court, asking to see the king. In doing so, she was literally taking her life into her hands since protocol demanded that she be summoned by the king. When the king saw her, he said, "What is it, Queen Esther? What is your request? Even up to half the kingdom, it will be given to you" (Esther 5:3 NIV).

By the way, I think this is a very telling remark, given the rule about being put to death if you entered the inner court without being summoned by the king. The king must have genuinely loved Esther. The fact that he offered her half of his kingdom as she stood there, vulnerable and uninvited, is mind-blowing. Anyway, her answer to his lofty offer was, "Baby, I just missed you and was wondering if you would like to come to a banquet I've prepared just for you. Oh, by the way, bring your friend Haman along." (I'm paraphrasing of course.) This woman was no ordinary female. Think of how many women would have jumped at the king's offer and forgotten why they came in the first place. Any one of us might have been flattered into convenient amnesia.

The next words out of the king's mouth were, "Bring Haman at once, so we can do what Esther asks." Did you hear that? He said "at once"! The king and Haman went to the banquet. While they were drinking wine, the king asked her again, "Esther, what is it, baby? What can I do for you? Whatever it is, up to half of the kingdom, it is yours for the asking, just say the word."

All she replied was, "Honey, all I ask is, if you love me, and if you really do want to give me the desire of my heart, the only thing I want from you is another visit. Let me prepare another banquet for you and your friend Haman again tomorrow. Then, I will answer your question." Now you've got to hand it to her, that was smooth. I would have been a nervous wreck and spilled the beans the minute he asked. But she was cool. She waited for God to perform. And perform He did.

That night, the king couldn't sleep so he had some of the chronicles of his reign read to him. He discovered that Mordecai had exposed a plot on his life, and that he had forgotten to reward him. Enter Haman (talk about perfect timing). The king solicits his advice for a suitable reward to honor someone who delights him. Haman, thinking it had to be himself, gives him some wonderful suggestions. Imagine how sick Haman felt when he realized he had suggested a reward that he now had to provide for his worst enemy! Hardly a suitable appetizer before his dinner with Esther and the king.

If the earlier part of the day was no fun, the evening got even worse. Here we are, back at dinner with the king, Haman, and Esther. Again, the king asked her, "Sweetheart, what can I do for you? I'll do it. What do you want? Up to half of the kingdom and it's yours." (This is the kind of man I'm looking for!)

Esther says, "Well, if you insist, and if I've found favor with you, if it really does please you, I need you to grant me my life. This is all I ask. And please spare my people who have been sold for destruction, annihilation, and slaughter. Now, if we were merely going to be sold as slaves, I wouldn't have brought it up because that would not have been a big enough distress to justify disturbing your majesty. . . . "

From that point on, stuff hit the fan! The king wanted to know who would do such a thing to his precious Esther. When Esther revealed that it was Haman who had plotted it, the king had to take a walk to cool off. By now Haman was delirious with fear, and thinking about throwing himself on Queen Esther's mercy. He threw himself on her couch instead. When the king returned from the garden and saw Haman falling all over Esther, that was the final straw.

He said, "No, you won't put your hands all over my lady, in my house, in my presence." On that note, the king decided he couldn't tolerate Haman any longer. Haman was hung on the gallows he had constructed to kill Mordecai.

The king gave Esther Haman's estate as a gift. But Esther wasn't finished. She fell at his feet, weeping and begged him to end the evil plan to kill the Jews because she could not bear to see her people destroyed. The king responded and ordered that an edict be issued according to her and Mordecai's instructions, granting the Jews the right to assemble and protect themselves. Because of this, many were converted to Judaism, because fear of the Jews seized the surrounding nationalities.

In the end, on the appointed day, the Jews struck down their enemies and destroyed them. When the report reached the king, he turned to Esther and said, "Baby, what else can I do for you?" And she, being the perfect lady, merely answered, "If it pleases you, let the Jews finish the job." And the king ordered it done. After that the kingdom ran peacefully, Esther and Mordecai established a holiday to celebrate what God had done, end of story.

Speaking the Truth in Love

These Bible stories may seem a little over the top in the face of simple issues you might want to relate to your man. But the principles are the same. When these simple principles are utilized, they will work miracles in any relationship: be a good listener, wait to speak, and give God room to act.

How could Abigail and Esther be so cool in the face of life-threatening situations? They looked beyond their own immediate danger and saw God's cause being tampered with. They had the assurance that He would intervene because it affected His kingdom agenda.

Now ask yourself a question. On any issue you find important enough to present to the man in your life, do you stop to think if it's a selfish request on your part? Is it something that God would be concerned about in the light of kingdom business? It's simple enough to figure out. Is your situation or concern addressed in Scripture? Is that Scripture being violated? If it is, then kingdom business is being affected, and you can trust God to intervene.

When you present your opinions and requests, do you speak the truth in love? Is your speech always with grace, seasoned with salt, with life-preserving words? It's not *what* you say, but *how* you say it that makes the difference. Consider Jezebel versus Abigail: same situation, very different conclusions. Men respond to needs, not to demands. This is a hard lesson for many a "liberated" woman to learn. But the evidence is there. For every woman in need, there will be a man somewhere close by being moved by her need. Men like to fix things, it's in their nature. It gives them the chance to rise to the occasion and be men.

Do you take the time to listen? Are you willing to really hear what the other person is saying? There's an old aphorism that we've been given two ears, but only one mouth. There is a similar rule in sales: The first person to speak loses the upper hand on the deal. Are you so lost in the land of "me" that you don't hear what the other person is asking or telling you? Did you notice that Esther didn't do a whole lot of talking? She left room for the king to make an offer. She didn't miss her opportunity to get what she wanted because she was not monopolizing the conversation, even though what she had on her mind was extremely important.

Do you wait for God to act on your behalf? Timing is everything. At the end of a hard day, before dinner, is *not* a good time to launch into what you want, what you need, what you've got to have. Save it for a quality quiet time when there is nothing else screaming for attention (and that includes empty stomachs). As one of my favorite Scriptures says, "There is a time for everything, and a season for every activity under heaven . . . a time to tear and a time to mend, a time to be silent and a time to speak" (Ecclesiastes 3:1,7).

Jesus, the Communicator

We should also follow Jesus' example in communication. When people approached Him with their concerns, He asked them a lot of questions. Instead of plunging in and giving them an immediate answer, He would ask them more questions. Although this was the methodology of Jewish teachers, I think Jesus knew a very important secret: There's something to be said for letting the other person arrive at the right conclusion.

If people make decisions based on the heart instead of the ears, the effect will be much more significant. If they carry out your requests just because you asked, it will be done halfheartedly. But if they arrive at the conviction that your request or need has validity, it will be fulfilled with fervor. "The king's heart is in the hand of the LORD, like the rivers of water; he turns it wherever He wishes" (Proverbs 21:1).

It is vitally important to understand that *it is God who creates favor for us in the hearts of man,* not us.

Another communication method Jesus used was to paint word pictures. He always met the people where they lived, and He spoke to them on their level. When He talked with farmers, He used farming illustrations to get his point across. When He spoke with fishermen and told them He would make them "fishers of men," they not only understood what that meant, but also had a feel for what it would entail to bring souls to the kingdom of God. For example, it would require selecting the proper bait and being willing to wait for the person to take hold of it. Then knowing when to pull, and being sensitive to the right amount of pressure to draw the person to the Lord.

Word pictures are effective because they enable you to speak the other person's language. They ensure that both of you are on the same page, in the same book. It sets the groundwork for total understanding and a fruitful exchange. Learning the fundamentals of what your future mate is involved in will help you use examples and situations he can relate to and understand.

The Bottom Line

Most important of all, know and have a clear understanding of what your needs are *before* you approach others with them. This is especially true when communicating with males. Men get very frustrated when the problem keeps changing. Remember, they are fixers. So if you just need a listening ear and not necessarily advice, state that up-front before he gets started. Otherwise, after you've dismissed several of his solutions, he will shut down, and your next complaint will be that he never listens to you.

Most women naturally like to massage their problems, turn them over, and examine them thoroughly before actively dealing with them. To most men, a problem is an opportunity for them to fix something, finish it, then move on. If you're still in the mull stage of a problem, discuss it with "the girls." They enjoy and understand the process a whole lot more. Also remember that a man's ego will be affected by how you react to his advice, so don't ask for his advice if you're not going to consider following it.

Sometimes it's hard to know exactly what's in our hearts, why we feel the way we do, and what we really need. Don't be quick to ignore the Mighty Counselor because there's a man in your life. There will be times when he, in his humanness, will not have a solution for you. But the Holy Spirit "helps in our weaknesses. For we do not know what we should pray for as we ought, but the Spirit Himself makes intercession for us with groanings which cannot be uttered. Now He who searches the hearts knows what the mind of the Spirit is, because He makes intercession for the saints according to the will of God" (Romans 8:26,26).

God is able to shine the light on our emotions. He can tell us what is going on with us better than anyone. He always gives the right advice and answers we need in a way that will surpass our expectations.

What is the most important key to communication with a mate, a friend, or even God? Openness. There is a story in Mark 7, starting at verse 32, that illustrates God's insight:

> There some people brought to him [Jesus] a man who was deaf and could hardly talk, and they begged him to place his hand on the man. After he took him aside, away from the crowd, Jesus put his fingers into the man's ears. Then he spit and touched the man's tongue. He looked up to heaven and with a deep sigh said to him "Ephphatha!" (which means, "Be opened!"). At this, the man's ears were opened, his tongue was loosened and he began to speak plainly.

This man's hearing had an effect on his ability to speak. Jesus touched his ears first!

Listening, Learning, and Being Vulnerable

In counseling training, a method called "empathic listening" is taught. A counselor is taught to mirror back what the other person has said. For instance, "I was so angry when she said that to me" would garner this response, "It sounds as if what she said really upset you." Which would result in this kind of exchange: "Yes, because what she said was not true." "So you feel that you were the victim of a lie." "Exactly! And it really hurt my feelings . . . you know, I didn't realize it until now, but, I'm more hurt than angry. I guess I felt betrayed." (A conclusion is not always reached as quickly as this, but you get the idea.)

Empathic listening is a good technique to sharpen your listening skills. It stops you from preparing your responses before you have heard everything the other person has to say. If you are already preparing a response in your head before the other person has finished stating his case, you are not remaining open. This can lead to misunderstanding and even greater division. Take the time to listen to the other person, and don't cling to your own response so fiercely that you are distracted from the point. If your position is true and important, it will pour from your heart when it's your turn to speak.

After Jesus had spit and touched his tongue and commanded "Ephphatha!" the man's ears were opened and his tongue was loosened. He was healed. There was a chain reaction. After the man was able to hear he was able to speak plainly—to communicate effectively in a way that resulted in complete understanding by the hearer. Understanding brings healing and reconciliation. This should be the goal of any exchange we have with others.

Jesus touched the man's tongue with his own saliva. This was an intimate exchange, a kiss, so to speak, a healing exchange, no higher, no lower than the other person. While you are making the decision to actively listen, don't entertain feelings of superiority. And, above all else, stay open to change.

Last but not least, avoid communication killers: anger, pride, secrecy, judgmental attitudes, and contentiousness. Proverbs 17:18 NIV says, "He who loves a quarrel loves sin; he who builds a high gate invites destruction." Don't shut yourself off. Always go to the source of pain, trouble, or misunderstanding. God will give you both the grace to impart healing and reconciliation to one another.

Also, try not to nurse and rehearse the situation too much with others. This only adds fuel to the fire and makes forgiveness and understanding a harder goal to accomplish. It serves to harden the hearts of yourself and others. Remember that "he who covers a transgression seeks love, but he who repeats a matter separates the best of friends" (Proverbs 17:9).

I encourage you to be open, to love enough to be vulnerable. Be gently honest. Anticipate healing. Make reconciliation your goal. Jesus did. Be willing to lay down your life, your pride, the "I," the "me" of your existence to make a stronger "we." It's not an "I'm okay, you're okay" attitude, but an honest appraisal, a "what can we do to make us work" philosophy. I believe this is the ultimate challenge, the reason why "two becoming one" is such a mystery. Fortunately, with the help of God the mystery can be solved.

14
The Initial Surrender

Whatever happened to superwoman?
    somewhere between
        juggling a career
           and womanhood
              she got lost
        beneath a stack of "do" lists
           endless appointments
           buried desires
    and accumulated achievements . . .

Whatever happened to superwoman?
    last seen tipping
        right off the balancing beam
      thrown off-kilter by too much weight
        carried in over-ambitious arms
    it has been reported
        that she lost the ability
        to walk between the raindrops
           without getting drenched . . .
        no longer able to move
           faster than the speed of sound
           emotionally

and physically spent
she maintained her image
stifling the urge to cry help
staggering onward
getting wetter and wetter
moving closer
to the kryptonite
of needs ignored
superwoman slipped
and fell . . .
into a puddle of wordless pride
that threatened to drain
the last strain of
independent strength
that she possessed . . .

Whatever happened to superwoman?
I found her crying disillusioned tears
weary of her own superhuman efforts
staring back at me
from the looking glass
begging me to keep her secret . . .
our secret . . .
that against all better efforts and judgment
the truth remained the same . . .
we were not created
to be alone
standing as miniature islands
flexing imaginary muscles
ignoring our hearts
our souls
our very essence . . .

Whatever happened to superwoman?
she unraveled her cape
in the face of understanding
and welcomed the Son
with open arms

vulnerable
unchallenging
growing ever stronger
in the celebration
of her weaknesses
she gave into love
and all that it brings
and found it much easier to fly . . .

It sounds good in theory, but the superwoman myth promotes a very dangerous line of thinking. It suggests that we can all make it on our own, independent of the help of others. For one thing, it would take superhuman strength for us to be totally independent. For another, independence without balance is rebellion, and rebellion always leads us on a path to self-destruction.

Dependent, Independent, Interdependent

Imagine a world filled with all chiefs and no Indians, each individual making decisions that affect the world, independent of one another. With that kind of arrangement, the world would end in an hour. Closer to home, envision a kitchen filled with cooks hovering over one pot, all preparing one soup, each adding favorite ingredients without consulting the others. I think the explosion in that kitchen would give a nuclear test bombing a run for its money.

We all long to be independent. From the moment we come out of our mother's womb we begin fighting for the right to be independent, to have our own way. But what are we really fighting for? Independence, according to Webster, is "not subject to control by others; self governing; not affiliated with a larger controlling unit; not requiring or relying on something else; not looking to others for one's opinions or for guidance in conduct; refusing to accept help from or to be under obligation to others."

If this is what is happening in your life, are you having fun yet? Small wonder women seem to have so many health problems these days. Their bodies are breaking down under the stress to maintain an independent, superwoman existence. This was never God's design.

Independent versus dependent versus codependent. We bounce these terms around more casually than we ought. The bottom line is that God designed us to be interrelated and *dependent* on Him and on one another. We humans were designed to function as one body. Those in the body of Christ are to have a deeper understanding of how this works:

> The body is a unit, though it is made up of many parts; and though all its parts are many, they form one body. . . . If the foot should say, "Because I am not a hand, I do not belong to the body," it would not for that reason cease to be part of the body. And if the ear should say, "Because I am not an eye, I do not belong to the body," it would not for that reason cease to be part of the body. If the whole body were an eye, where would the sense of hearing be? If the whole body were an ear, where would the sense of smell be? But in fact God has arranged the parts in the body, every one of them, just as he wanted them to be. . . .
>
> The eye cannot say to the hand, "I don't need you!" And the head cannot say to the feet, "I don't need you!" . . .
>
> But God has combined the members of the body and has given greater honor to the parts that lacked it, so that there should be no division in the body, but that its parts should have equal concern for each other. If one part suffers, every part suffers with it; if one part is honored, every part rejoices with it" (1 Corinthians 12:12,15-18,21,24-26).

Can you imagine what would happen if each body part decided to do its own thing and work independently of all the others? When the body is in a healthy state, all of the body parts cooperate with one another and take orders from one center, the brain. The brain lets every part know what it's going to do, and those parts move accordingly. When the brain isn't working, when something short circuits its signals, the body is thrown out of order. The normal functions that should be second nature are either paralyzed or thrown out of whack. These types of symptoms are usually diagnosed under the heading of debilitating diseases.

When we're independent of other parts of the body of Christ, we end up with ulcers, high blood pressure, and other unhealthy conditions. We were not meant to function outside the body of Christ.

The Liberating Power of Submission

Where am I heading? We are on our way toward our—yours and mine—favorite subject: submission. You didn't really think we would get all the way through this book without talking about it did you? Whether you're single, in the midst of courtship, or married, submission is crucial to your health—spiritually, mentally, emotionally, and physically.

One of my favorite authors and a personal friend, Philomina "Bunny" Wilson, said it best when she entitled one of her books *Liberated Through Submission*. I know this may be shockingly contrary to the way you've been programmed up to this point. It certainly goes against the world's view. But there is something unbelievably freeing about submission.

I would like to propose a new way of thinking about submission. Submission was designed to free you from bearing the burden and the responsibilities of life alone. It's that simple. It was not designed to insult you as a woman, or to suggest that you are less than anyone else, or to rob you of opportunity. Submission is crucial to the order of kingdom living.

Even God submits to us. He gave us free will; he doesn't override our choices. He doesn't force Himself or His will on us. If we choose to accept or reject Him, He submits to our choice.

That doesn't mean He gives up on us, He simply waits until we allow Him in. He doesn't like all of the choices that we make, but He allows us to take the journey we've chosen, patiently watching over us until we arrive back at His throne in a position of surrender. Are you able to submit like that with your friends and loved ones? I think we all have a lot to learn about submission.

For those of you who cringe at the word, why do you have no problem with the Scriptures "submit to God" (James 4:7), or "all of you be submissive to one another, and be clothed with humility, for 'God resists the proud, but gives grace to the humble'" (1 Peter 5:5)? And why do you go ballistic the moment someone whispers, "Wives, submit to your own husbands, as to the Lord" (Ephesians 5:22)? It might be because Satan knows that "a house divided against itself will not stand" (Matthew 12:25). If all the time spent in a relationship is focused on competition, how will you move forward as a couple?

God designed marriage to be a living, breathing example of the hierarchy of heaven. In heaven, there are levels of authority. God is at the head and everything works outward from Him. Even among the angels there are levels of authority: angels, archangels, cherubim, and seraphim. God's perfect design of order means that no one in the kingdom is overloaded with his or her duties.

How can you break out of the superwoman syndrome? The first step is recognizing and admitting you need help. The second step is realizing your help lies in submission: submission to God, submission to others, submission to the mate that God provides.

Preparing for Submission

Whether or not you have someone in your life right now, you can find out how you feel about submission in your everyday living with God, who is presently filling the mate slot in your life. I was horrified one day when the Lord very gently told me, "You know, Michelle, being single is a lot easier for you than married life is going to be. That's because you can always slide out of doing what I tell you since you have no physical mani-festation of me to face." Talk about a rude awakening! How could I argue with Him? He was right, like He always is.

I realized I had become a little drunk with my own power over my life. I went where I wanted, did what I wanted, bought what I wanted, whenever and wherever I chose. Without a back-ward glance or afterthought, I lived life full-force, filled with self-indulgent delight. I owed it to myself, or so I thought. It was my reward for having to live life alone. Small wonder my male friends who were honest with me considered me high-maintenance and unaffordable.

Back on my knees I went, feeling quite contrite, realizing the full meaning of what my precious heavenly Father had told me. I knew that some of those self-indulgent habits would be very hard to break, even if I tried to break them for the man I loved. I mean, let's face it, I would still want what I wanted. Being in love wasn't going to get rid of my love for shoes, for instance. Was I going to be able to happily ignore a fabulous shoe sale in order to stick to a family budget? At this stage, quite honestly, the answer was no. Very tentatively I agreed to submit my lifestyle to the Lord.

He took me up on it right away. The next day as I was strolling through one of my favorite stores (it was a shortcut on my way home, don't you know), I noticed a silver bracelet that I had been lusting after had gone on sale. All the more reason to purchase it now, I thought. So I swooped over to the counter and claimed my little prize.

Before I could turn to walk away from the saleslady, the Lord said to me, "Take it back." That's when the fight began. I knew if I walked around the store long enough, God would change His mind. But guess what? He didn't. The closer I got to the exit, the sicker I felt. I could feel Him watching me cling to my package in outright rebellion. I couldn't take it, so back to the counter I slithered. In a very small voice I told the saleslady, "I'm sorry, but my 'husband' has asked me to return this." She looked perplexed, but I felt quite relieved.

The Value of Listening

As it turned out, an emergency arose, and I needed every dime I would have spent on that bracelet. Because I was obedient, the money was there. This led me to realize something else about submission . . . it is for our own protection.

There was a scene in the movie *The Godfather III* that really struck me. Toward the end of the movie, the "godfather" tells his daughter he doesn't want her seeing the man she is in love with. The entire family is leaving a building together, and she breaks out of her place in the entourage to argue and plead with him. Meanwhile, an assassin is waiting to shoot him. You can guess the rest; she gets shot and dies instead. I remember how shaken I was. I said to myself over and over again, "If only she had stayed in her place and listened to her father."

I was raised on the words "because I said so" and, as a child, they infuriated me. Although I felt I was owed an explanation for their decisions about my life, my parents offered none except to remind me that they knew what was best. As I got older, I learned how many times those words were my safety net.

Because God says so, we must learn how to submit to Him without argument (whether it is His voice you hear or the voice of sound counsel from someone He has placed in your life). Sometimes it can be a matter of life or death.

We submit joyfully when we keep our eyes on Jesus in the midst of submitting. God is at the helm of whatever is going on in your life, and every single moment is being used to mold you and make you into the person He wants you to be. For instance, is your boss being difficult?

> Slaves, obey your earthly masters with respect and fear, and with sincerity of heart, just as you would obey Christ. Obey them not only to win their favor when their eye is on you, but like slaves of Christ, doing the will of God from your heart. Serve wholeheartedly, as if you were serving the Lord, not men, because you know that the Lord will reward everyone for whatever

good he does, whether he is slave or free (Ephesians 6:5-7 NIV).

God won't be able to deal with your boss if you're in the way, busy fighting your own battles. It has been my experience that when I am in right standing with Him, God moves on my behalf. But the more I rebel against authority, the harder the lessons of submission become.

Do I Trust This Man?

The ability to submit relies heavily on our capacity to trust and respect the person giving the orders or making the decisions. This is where choosing the right husband comes in. Ask yourself *before* you say yes to a serious relationship, Do I trust this man to make good decisions for me and our future family? Do I respect his walk with God and how he handles his affairs? How does he deal with authority? Is he able to submit? Don't let the candlelight and roses distract you. These are very important questions that should be answered affirmatively or there will be trouble ahead. Remember, the Word says, "Submit to one another in the fear of God" (Ephesians 5:21).

To be perfectly honest, the most difficult part of this arrangement falls on men. They are exhorted to love us as Christ loves the church. Now, I think I'm pretty lovable, but—even to me—that's asking a bit much. The man in my life has to love me unconditionally whether I'm being lovable or not! He has to be willing to give his life for me. He has to be totally self-sacrificing for my sake. He has to be responsible for me spiritually, emotionally, and physically. And if he doesn't treat me right . . . his prayers won't be answered. First Peter 3:7 (NIV) admonishes, "Husbands, in the same way be considerate as you live with your wives, and treat them with respect as the weaker partner and as heirs with you of the gracious gift of life, so that nothing will hinder your prayers."

Now before you get all upset and bent out of shape over the words "weaker partner," realize that Paul was not referring to intellect. He was referring to physical limitations. Structurally, men are usually stronger than women. And most of us women are not pumping iron at Gold's Gym or trying out for Miss Universe muscle competitions. We can still use a hand from time to time getting something open or carrying something that is a bit too heavy for us. Paul is merely reminding the menfolk to be gentlemen and treat us as the prizes we are. And isn't that what we really want? Of course, it goes deeper than that: God holds our mate totally responsible for our well being. That's a pretty tall order.

Women, however, are simply asked to submit. The Amplified version translates Ephesians 5:22 this way: "Wives, be subject (submissive and adapt yourselves) to your own husband as [a service] to the Lord. We are to fit in with our mate's plans. In other words, don't work against him, work with him, be a partner. If you've elected to spend your life with a man that you believe makes wise decisions, has a heart that is totally open to God's leading, and always seems to consider your needs, this should be an easy thing for you to do. Your willing submission to him will be merely an automatic response to his outpouring of love to you.

The secret to submission is understanding, and true understanding means you are able to stand under the other person's position or beliefs. It is in the "standing under" that you are covered and protected. Consider it an umbrella effect, shielding you from negative elements. If you believe that this man truly loves you and is always considerate of what's best for you, then you can believe that his decisions are not coming from a position of self-seeking indulgence. So stand under the protection and guidance that has been given to you through the mate God has selected for you.

If there is a point of dissension, don't be quick to decide that the one who has to change is your man. It might be you. Or it might be a matter of timing. In any case, the first person to be consulted when there is a disagreement is God. He will either change your man's heart or yours. I realize that in this independent world, this is revolutionary thinking, but you are working toward marriage, where God will expect you to move as one. The only way to be united in mind is to be united in spirit.

Realities About Gender

God has His reasons for selecting the man to be head over the woman. "For Adam was formed first, then Eve. And Adam was not deceived, but the woman being deceived, fell into transgression" (1 Timothy 2:13,14). That may not sit well with you, but it's the truth.

Eve was deceived, while Adam ate the fruit deliberately. He knew the cost of partaking of the fruit, but he also knew the cost of not eating it—separation from Eve. He chose Eve over God at that moment. Don't tell me women aren't powerful! Women, let's use our power for good, to inspire our men to heightened states of godliness.

Among others, men and women have two distinctly different but equally powerful gifts. Women have the gift of spiritual instinct. They can sense danger, among other things, from miles away. They just have a knowing down deep inside their beings that doesn't rely on intellectual fact. And, much to the dismay of their partners, they are right most of the time. Women are, however, vulnerable to emotion, which can cloud their perception.

Men, on the other hand, view things with a clarity that is not distracted by emotion. They survey the facts, tally up the bottom line, and make their moves based totally on reason. But sometimes reason alone can dismiss important spiritual implications. This is why either of these modes of operation can be handicapped when in operation alone. The two gifts when combined, form a strong defense against evil.

These two gifts are the personification of the Scripture "the letter kills, but the Spirit gives life" (2 Corinthians 3:6). The letter of the law is needed as foundational guidance, but the spirit brings understanding and extends the revelation of what God has dictated. It breathes life into the words on the page.

Both facets of God's truth are needed: the letter and the Spirit. They work like thunder and lightning. Thunder is the noise that lightning makes. The lightning strikes first, and the sound of thunder follows. That is the order, and they never work apart from one another. They do not exist apart from one another. And together, the combination is powerful. God did not create man or woman to dominate the other. Each gender was created to complement and help the other.

Teamwork requires that everyone on the team be in submission to the other in order to win the game. Everyone must be willing to pass the baton. The man you're involved with, if he is truly sold out to God, will know when to listen to you. He will also know when to lovingly stand firm in what God has instructed him to do, even when it doesn't line up with what you believe or feel. And if you truly have a heart for God, you will trust his ability to hear God, and you will rest in God's direction for both of you. It's called give and take.

In a world where respect for authority seems to be fading, this may be a hard line of thinking for you. But remember, everything that God says in His Word was designed to make our lives the best they can be. He has designed an entire universe that works in harmony and submission to its myriad of elements. The sun doesn't argue with the moon and demand the right to shine longer. Each takes its turn rising and setting. The seasons run their course in the time they are allotted. Even the animals in nature follow their own unspoken rules. How much more can we, who have the mind of Christ, work together to reflect the kingdom of God to others by working toward a relationship that functions in mutual respect and harmony?

Why don't you give your man—your future husband—some room to rise to the occasion of being the man that God has called him to be. After you're married he will be your spiritual head, your protector. Your provider, your lover. Your friend. Take a chance and just enjoy being a woman covered and loved by your future mate. He will have a wonderful sense of self and so will you. And isn't it ultimately more fun to think up ways to please your man than to plot how to gain the upper hand?

Increasing and Decreasing

Which leads us back full circle to the first order of submission: Submit to God. Submit to His plans for your life. Submit to His time schedule. We don't always like what God puts on our plates, but because we've chosen to trust Him with our hearts and our lives, we receive what He gives. Sometimes the things God allows in our lives are hard, but the outcome is based on how we choose to deal with what we've been given. We can become resistant, hard, and unfruitful. Or we can submit to the lesson, blossom from the learning, and bear the kind of fruit that makes our heavenly Father proud. The choice is ours.

I've always looked at marriage as a college course—Christianity 202. It is where we get to practice living in the kingdom. As John the Baptist so wisely put it, "[The Lord] must increase, but I must decrease" (John 3:30). The more God increases in our lives, the more He is glorified.

People are always watching us, so our lives are always shaping someone's opinion about God and what it means to be a Christian. The most apparent witness to those around us is how we submit or yield to others. When we yield to the people God has placed around us, we give God the right of way to clarify, rectify, or nullify our situation. Just as in traffic situations, if no one yields, someone gets hurt.

Not long ago, I was crossing the street at a corner. A driver was stopped at a stop sign. I clearly had the right of way. Just as I crossed the front of his car, he stepped on the gas, and I was badly injured. After three operations on my knee and almost a year of therapy, I am finally on the road to recovery, but the scar that remains is a fear of crossing the street. I'm still afraid the cars won't stop.

Sometimes we feel blindsided when the people we love do not cooperate with us. We fail to see that a lack of cooperation may be tough love for us on their part. The no's in our lives are placed there as detours that allow us to learn valuable, character-shaping lessons—lessons that put us on the road to God's plan for our lives. When we fail to yield or to pay attention to the signs, personal collisions and "life" jams occur. While we are left to weep over the destruction, Satan is delighted with the confusion and injury he has caused.

Selfish people are reckless drivers on the road of life. You've seen them weaving in and out of traffic, and wondered how long it would take them to cause an accident. Submission, like communication, is geared toward reconciliation and seeking the best for us and for the people in our lives. That's why it is important to remember that it is no longer you or me, "but it's Christ in us. "It is God who works in you both to will and to do for His good pleasure" (Philippians 2:13). Not *your* good pleasure, *God's* good pleasure. If you insist on your own way, you are not the only one who loses—God's kingdom does, too.

The beautiful thing about submission is that we have a choice. Let's choose life (obedience) over death (rebellion). Let's decide to submit to God, submit to our authorities, submit to our mates, submit to love.

15
The First Revelation

Yes, this is love—demanding, nourishing, and difficult. Yet it possesses the ability to make us wiser and stronger than we ever dreamed. As we've discovered, there are innumerable treasures to be gained from mastering the art of commitment, for staying when you would rather leave, for pressing upward when, ultimately, it would be easier to lay down on the job. So when love comes, allow it in and resist the urge to turn away. Even though love will always ask for that which you are afraid to give—give it anyway. You see, true love will always demand that you stretch beyond where you have ever been. As the popular Nike ad says, "Just do it."

Destroying the Marriage Idol

In the face of all that love is and all that it demands, we must make an honest assessment and decision about any potential mate. In order to do this, we must tear down the idols concerning love and marriage. Throughout the Old Testament, whenever the people erected idols in the high places, trouble followed. Kings who were wise knew that in order to have the blessing of God, all other idols and gods had to be removed from the land. So the high places and the groves were leveled, the abominations to God were removed, and peace prevailed for a time. Then, slowly but surely, the rules were relaxed. One by one the idols reappeared, and havoc eventually followed.

Today, there are high places in our hearts and our minds. We go through seasons where we, too, have the best of intentions. Our hopes for marriage don't seem as urgent, and we are in a state of contentment. Happily we hum, "I am happy and blessed, watching and waiting, looking above, wrapped in His goodness, lost in His love." Then all of a sudden an old aunt comes to town and asks the dreaded question: "So why aren't you married yet?" Up go the idols, and we are propelled into a state of discontentment. We begin to question God, question ourselves and, in the process, lose our peace and our discernment. We begin to focus on finding a man instead of keeping our focus on God.

This is when many women, including godly women, begin to make very foolish choices. They jump into relationships and marriages prematurely in a desperate attempt to validate their desirability. They find themselves in a befuddled state shortly after the honeymoon, their dreams in shambles around their feet, and feeling the weight of the vows they promised God they would keep. This becomes fertile ground for the enemy to cultivate a crop of unvictorious thoughts and self-defeating actions.

"Why didn't I see him for what he was?"

"Why did I have so many misguided expectations?"

"Why am I still not happy, still not fulfilled?"

These are some of the questions women ask after they've allowed marriage to became an idol in their hearts and have gone the distance in giving their lives over to that idol. They find out that "something" is not always better than "nothing." But they find out too late.

I encourage you to tear down the idols and "wait on the LORD, and keep his way, and he shall exalt thee to inherit the land" (Psalm 37:34 KJV). Don't let the pressures around you make you settle for anything less than God's will for your life.

In the book of 1 Samuel, King Saul let the people pressure him into not waiting for God's anointed to offer the sacrifice after a battle. It cost him his kingdom. Don't allow impatience and the expectations of others to rob you of the kingdom of happiness, growth, and fulfillment that God is preparing for you.

Heading for God's High Places

One of my favorite books is a classic by Hannah Hurnard called *Hinds Feet on High Places*. The central character, Much Afraid, longs to go to the High Places and experience true love. She has some physical deficiencies that make this difficult. Nevertheless, the Shepherd assures her it is possible, and she sets off on an event-filled journey.

She is pursued by Pride, Bitterness, and a number of other unsavory characters who are bent on hindering her progress. Finally, against all odds, she reaches her destination. However, to her chagrin, she discovers that in order to experience true love, she has to completely release her desire for love.

This proves to be difficult and painful because wanting to be loved is so firmly entrenched within her. But her desire to be free and pleasing to the Shepherd is stronger than the desires that bind her. She releases her heart into the hands of the Shepherd, and receives true love in place of the old desires for human acceptance that she had held so dear. Also, a pleasant surprise awaited her. She was transformed! Her physical deficiencies were healed. She was a completely whole person, ready to serve the Shepherd.

Much Afraid's journey is very similar to ours. She wandered aimlessly by the Sea of Loneliness, descended down to the Valley of Despair—all the usual pit stops we make. She allowed the voices of the enemies of her soul to cause her to doubt and stumble. She eventually made it—and so will we. But, like her, we must yield to the process of transformation, allowing the idols associated with finding love to be removed from our hearts.

Bright, Shining Lamps

Every moment spent waiting is a valuable time of prepara-tion. We should be in a state of continual readiness. We should not be like the foolish young virgins on their way to the wed-ding feast who took their lamps but took no oil (see Matthew 25). While the bridegroom tarried, they slept. When his arrival was announced, they had no oil in their lamps. While they searched for oil, the bridegroom came and those who were ready with their lamps burning bright went in to the marriage feast. By the time they got themselves together, the foolish ones were locked out.

Is there oil in your lamp? Now is your time to shine! Embrace life for all its worth. Drink in God's wisdom, and savor all the experiences He offers you. As a single woman, you can prepare yourself to be a rich and brilliant addition to your mate. Learn all you can about love and giving by exercising it where you are, with the people God has put in your life right now.

Relationship skills are not acquired overnight. Don't fool yourself into thinking that the moment you fall in love you will automatically acquire all the traits required to make a relation-ship work smoothly. Begin to work out the kinks in the rela-tionships you already have. Friends, parents, coworkers, and siblings provide a wide array of opportunities to practice uncon-ditional love, selflessness, and problem-solving exercises. These will prepare you for a lifetime of service to the man of God's choice for you.

Relaxing in the Everlasting Arms

"Fine," you're saying, "but why is this taking so long? What is keeping the Lord from granting me this one heartfelt desire?" I don't know. Who can understand the mind of Christ or His purposes? But this much I do know: There is a place in single-ness with Christ that is surprisingly sweet. It is a place where we can feel completed, surrounded by His love, and covered in His care. And it is like nothing we will ever experience with another human being.

One night I dreamed that I was looking for my mate. Every time I reached the place where I thought he was, I was told I had just missed him. Finally, I grew weary. So I went to my father's house and fell asleep. When I woke up the man I had been looking for was there, standing silently, watching me sleep, waiting for me! The dream reminded me of something I already knew—while we wait, we should relax.

We should even relax when we feel discouraged. I used to try to keep a stiff upper lip and pretend I didn't mind being alone. The more I clenched my fists against the pain, the deeper I hurt. It was as if I were in quicksand, the more I wiggled, the deeper I sank. So I finally relaxed in the arms of my Savior. I told Him that I was lonely and hurting.

Soon I noticed that the more I accepted the reality of good days and bad days, the more the bad days subsided. I stopped beating myself up and decided to roll with the punches. Along the way, I made a startling discovery. My painful, lonely days were the days I focused on myself. The days I spent reaching out to those around me, pouring out love, and ministering to their needs were the richest days of my existence.

Yes, from time to time I still have my negative moments. Every now and then I look at my watch or my calendar, and lift an eyebrow to the sky. But deep in my heart I know that my Redeemer lives, and He knows what's best for me. I also know that after all is said and done, and after watching what some people have had to bear in their marriages, I want to wait for a God-ordained match, sent from heaven's golden chambers.

So, no matter how unpleasant it might seem from time to time, wait I will. . . .

> *I have watched*
> *and waited*
> *for my knight*
> *to come riding over the hill*

of my desires . . .
watching . . .
waiting . . .
to see him
dressed in white
upon a horse
big and strong
as his shoulders
where I will lay my head
as he carries me away
to the promised land
of dreams come true
and joy eternal . . .
watching . . .
waiting
peering from the window
of my fortress
my rock
my strong tower
with my heart in God's hands
left there for safe keeping
I peek expectantly
over my Father's shoulder
every now and then
settling back into the warmth of His lap
I watch . . .
I wait . . .
trusting that my expectation
will arrive
beautiful
resplendent
covered in the dew
that falls from heaven
being all that I hoped for
better than I dreamed
loving me
the way I want to be loved

freely
unconditionally
adoring me
as if I were
the best thing since sliced bread . . .
you know
that when-a-man-loves-a-woman
how-Christ-loves-the-church kinda love
too high
too deep
for me to truly comprehend
but it sure sounds good to me . . .
so I watch
and I wait
sometimes feeling like Rapunzel
sometimes Sleeping Beauty. . . .
waiting . . .
waiting
sometimes conscious
sometimes not
hope keeping the light shining
like a beacon in my eyes
beckoning my knight
should he lose his way
but for now
I lay content in the arms of my Savior
letting Him rock me
and love me
like no other lover can . . .
and I learn of love
of life
and giving . . .
and I wait . . .
clear-eyed
with no misguided expectations
no desperate desires
no distorted views

> *binding me*
> *marring my judgment*
> *I am free*
> *to say yes*
> *to say no*
> *according to the King's leading*
> *in spite of my flesh*
> *or my heart*
> *only a God-appointed knight*
> *will I receive*
> *no matter how long the wait*
> *I will wait . . .*
> *I will wait for Him . . .*

For a long time, John the Baptist had been saying, "The kingdom of God is at hand!" Imagine the joy he felt when Jesus arrived on the scene. All that he had been waiting and hoping for seemed to have manifested itself. Still he was cautious. He sent His disciples to Jesus to ask, "Are You the Coming One, or should we look for another?" (Matthew 11:3).

Jesus sent back a message describing the miracles that had been taking place in the course of His ministry. He added, "Blessed is he who is not offended because of me" (Matthew 11:6). The Amplified version states, "Blessed (happy, fortunate, and to be envied) is he who takes no offense at Me and finds no cause for stumbling in or through Me and is not hindered from seeing the Truth."

In similar terms, blessed is the woman who doesn't allow her desire for a man to cause her to stumble or hinder her from seeing the truth. We should always check a man's spiritual fruit against the Word of God. Make an honest assessment, even if it is a painful one. In this matter of life or heartbreak, we can't afford to let our desire for marriage blind us.

Let's not be so quick to proclaim, "This is him!" just because a dove lands on his head. Satan can produce signs, too. We should examine the man's ministry to us and to the other people around him. Is he the kind of man God told us to expect? Are we in a free and relaxed state, willing to hold out for God's best?

Let's take our time. After all, we're discussing the rest of our lives here. If we've been single this long, a little extra time to make sure it's the right relationship is nothing in the grand scheme of things. Let's take the time to observe, to be counseled, to ask lots and lots of questions—and *really listen* to the answers. These are life-saving measures. Let's treat this man as if he were applying for a job. Is he qualified to be a husband spiritually, emotionally, and financially? Are we willing to take everything we think we want, lay it on the altar, and set a match to it—and tell God we want what *He* wants for us? That's what it takes in order to make sound decisions in the face of what looks like clear evidence of delivered dreams.

I used to get so angry when friends told me, "You have to be happy with just the Lord before He will give you your mate." I thought that was so selfish on God's part. Today I know it's the most protective measure He could ever take on my behalf or yours. He knows that desperation breeds bad decisions, decisions that can hurt us deeply. It was never God's plan for the women in His court to be desperate. We are His daughters.

How do we arrive at the hallowed halls of satisfaction? I think we must mimic Much Afraid and give the Shepherd permission to remove our longing. I don't think we are capable of doing it ourselves but, somehow, when we give Him permission to do it for us, He is able.

I can't tell you the day or time it happened for me, I can only tell you that one day I rolled over on my pillow and murmured quite happily, "You know, Lord, it doesn't get any better than this. It's just me and You—how wonderful." Then I gasped as the impact of what I said hit me full force. I was happy, truly happy!

Nothing in my life had changed—except for my state of heart. This transformation had to be a supernatural work on God's part. I had struggled so hard and so long that I had simply exhausted myself, only to find that God had all the time in the world to wait for me to allow Him to free me. And you know what? Once I was free, I was also free to see my lack of readiness for what I had insisted I had to have all along.

Content with the Present

Whether we are married or single, happiness and fulfillment are not states that we can reach in our own power. The joy we all seek, the joy God offers, is completely independent of our living conditions and life situations. Many a married person feels lonely; many a single person is completely satisfied. There is something to be said for marriage and singleness—one is not lesser or greater than the other. But which mode would cause you to function at your greatest level? That is the question.

The time I've spent working through my life of singleness has caused me to dig deeper into God. I've had time to search for answers that seemed to elude not only me but also a great number of single sisters I've known. I have witnessed their struggles and chronicled my own. I have watched their reactions when they finally met someone and, in some instances, wed someone. I have laughed with them in their triumphs, wept with them in their failings. And most importantly, we have learned from each other.

Some of the answers I've discovered and offered to you are hard to accept. We would like an easier way out, a more instant sort of gratification. But that is not God's way. He doesn't believe in zapping us. Instead, He chooses to bring us through, out, and above our circumstances. His ways lead us to truth and life—and the truth is the light. The truth sets us free to rise above feelings of loneliness, rejection, and pain. The truth lifts us above the fear of facing the unknown alone, of not living out the American dream of a family with 2.5 children, a two-car garage, and a dog. The truth means we can cast all our cares on Him, for He cares for us (see 1 Peter 5:7).

The truth means we can trust God to deliver His best for us in His perfect timing. For those of you who still aren't so sure, or are, in the words of a popular author still, "waiting to exhale," inhale this: desperation and fear are like flypaper. It attracts all the wrong specimens and undesirable creatures. So don't lower your standards or settle for a "bitter thing" because you're looking at your watch. Trust me—a man seldom gets any sweeter after the wedding. However, if you let it be known that you refuse to settle for anything less than God's criteria for the man in your life, he can make the choice to rise to the occasion or fade out of the picture. You have the power to inspire and challenge that man to be all that God has called him to be if you believe God enough to keep your cool. After all, you haven't worked to become a "good woman" in order to get stuck with a "so-so man." Remember, sweet and sour only go together in Chinese food, not in real life. So be willing to wait. Only embrace a man who has a heart for God's purposes for his life and God's heart for you. Keep hope alive! Truly "all things are possible with God."

Choosing Mates "As Is"

Have you ever run across an item on sale marked "as is"? This means that the item must be bought and accepted in whatever condition we found it. Usually it has some sort of flaw, so we have to decide if we can live with it, flaw and all.

Once I saw a wonderful pair of white pants on sale for $1.99. Unfortunately, they had black grease stains all over them. I decided it was worth two dollars to see if I could get the grease out with stain remover. So I bought them. After a vigorous session of applying elbow grease, the stains came out. I was quite pleased with myself. I now had a wonderful pair of expensive slacks for two dollars! If only real life worked like that.

I may have put more thought into dealing with the flaws in those pants than some women put into their decision to live with the flawed man in their lives. The difference between men and my slacks are that changes with men don't come so easy, and sometimes not at all. Are we able to live with the fact that what we see is what we get?

Be honest. Whatever you do, don't imagine you can change a man or that all of a sudden the light will go on and he will immediately become a new person. Forget it! People generally are who they are. Any changes made will only be by the hand of God, and even those will take time. God is extremely patient; how patient are you?

Counting the Cost

Jesus admonishes us to consider the cost of being His disciple and following Him. "For which of you, intending to build a tower, does not sit down first, and count the cost, whether he has enough to finish it" (Luke 14:28). Notice it doesn't say whether he *will* have enough. Are you prepared now to make the commitment necessary to build a lasting relationship?

God is faithful in supplying all that we need. However, some situations we choose have little to do with Him, and everything to do with our own willfulness and desires. Because God's grace is so bountiful, He covers us even when we've invited our own disaster. Some situations just require good sense and if "any of you lacks wisdom, let him ask of God, who gives to all liberally and without reproach, and it will be given to him" (James 1:5). So get some wisdom, girlfriend. If the man you are dating cheats on you, what makes you think he won't cheat on you after you marry him? Remember, you have given him your stamp of approval by accepting him as he is. Is he irresponsible with money? Sloppy? Lazy? Whatever he is, if you settle, you are committed. I'm not trying to be negative here. This is simply a reality check. Is he what you really want? Is he what you *deserve?* No! No! A thousand times no! And God doesn't think so either.

I am deeply saddened at the muck and mire women in and out of the church are sinking into en masse. If you only knew how precious you are to God! What a valuable commodity you are! He loves you with an everlasting love! He wants to give you a physical manifestation of His love for you!

So learn how much you're worth to God. Revel in that information and then walk in it. Find out what love means to

God, and then expect and accept nothing less. Internalize His promises to you concerning a mate, then confess and stand on them. Stop having tea parties with Satan. Don't allow his lies to throw you into a state of distress no matter how long you've been waiting. Remember, *God's purpose prevails.* I know that it's really easy to get discouraged and fearful after reading statistics that say there are few good men left. That coupled with a sweeping calculation of how many of the men left are actively in relationship with the Lord, can make you desperate. Don't let it!

In 2 Kings 6, the king of Syria sent an army to outnumber the prophet Elisha. When his servant panicked, Elisha remained cool. He simply prayed for the Lord to open his servant's eyes and let him see the countless armies of the Lord outnumbering the Syrian army. Ask God to give you the ability to see that there are still good men left in this world. And, more importantly, that there is one for you! The bottom line is that if it is His will, God has your man safe and secure. He isn't going anywhere. God is diverting traffic. In the story from 2 Kings, Elisha also prayed that God would blind the eyes of the Syrian army. He then led them right to the capital city of Israel where the king made them prisoners of war. Pray that your future husband will have eyes only for you. God can agree and cooperate with that.

Just remember: When you meet this man, keep cool. It doesn't matter what you've heard about him, how cute he is, or what kind of car he drives. Be thorough in your examination before you give your heart away. We should follow the example of the Queen of Sheba. When she heard about Solomon, she went to see for herself. It says in 1 Kings 10 that she tested him with hard questions. After he had answered all of her questions with great wisdom because he received his answers from the Lord, she examined his character, his actions, then took in all of his material wealth and the countenance of those around him. Only then did she conclude that he had surpassed her expectations.

I confidently leave you with this very simple piece of information: No matter how long you have been waiting, the man God has for you will surpass your expectations. You will meet him when God says so. Not a minute early, not a moment late.

And as a King's daughter who has spent time in the King's court, it behooves you to carry out the proper courting etiquette. After all, you are a member of the royal family. Don't go in saying "Oh Lord, *please* let this be him." This is not a royal posture at all. Wait. Observe. Question. Let the man expose the hidden motives of his heart. Inhale . . . wait for God to give direction . . . exhale.

And then say, "*Yes!*"

A FINAL WORD

Shortly after I finished this book I had lunch with a group of friends. Eventually, the subject got around to one of our favorites: men. I was commenting on some of the rules our mothers taught us that had pretty much been discarded in the era of the "modern woman"—for example, "Girls never call boys—wait for them to come to you." Which is really saying the man should do all the work to win you and start a relationship.

One of my friends proceeded to give me a long list of reasons why she didn't agree with any of the general rules our mothers gave. "I don't like playing games," she said. "I like being open and giving to people I care about. Why should I have to go through all of that?"

At that point I stopped her. "Pamela, are you sure you aren't afraid to follow those suggestions because it means that a man will have to love you for simply being you . . . no cards, no gifts, no bells, no whistles . . . no performances to earn his love? It leaves you feeling kind of naked, doesn't it?"

On that note Pamela burst into tears and confessed she had been performing to earn love and approval all her life. It started with her parents and had crept into every other relationship.

This is a very common problem, especially at a time when the standards of beauty and desirability seem to be escalating to unreachable standards. Take a bucketful of low self-esteem and mingle it in with the world's expectations and you've got a quivering, hopeless mass of insecurity. We find ourselves jumping through endless hoops screaming "I'm gonna make you love me!" This is the devil's cleverest trick to set us up for repeated rejections that will leave our souls in shambles.

First John 4:19 says, "We love Him because He first loved us." Jesus loved us first. We hadn't done a thing to earn that love except exist. That's the scary part. There is nothing we can do to earn God's unconditional love. That kind of love is God's nature. It is also part of His design for marriage. The groom is to love his bride and give himself for her, just as Christ gave Himself for His people.

The most important message I can give you is: If God considered you lovable enough to give the life of His own Son for you, a mere mortal man should recognize your worth. Since God loves you, the man in your life should regard you as a "pearl of great price." He should be willing to follow God's plan and give his all for the precious gift of your affection.

You are beautiful. You are special. You are precious. You are lovable. All this, simply because you are. Simply because God says so. Believe it. Walk in the knowledge of it. Conduct yourself appropriately.

Dare to love yourself as God loves you and see what happens. Don't settle for less than His standard of love in your life. Say no to unloving counterfeits. Dare to wait for God's best. Dare to hope. Dare to dream. Dare to believe that you deserve to be loved. Dare to just be you—an incredibly loveable woman of God.

RECOMMENDED READING

Allen, Dr. Patricia and Harmon, Sandra. *Getting to "I Do."* William Morrow and Company.*

DeAngelis, Barbara, Ph.D. *Are You the One for Me?* Island Books.*

Fein, Ellen and Schneider, Sherrie. *The Rules.* Warner Publishing.*

Gray, John, Ph.D. *Men Are from Mars, Woman Are from Venus.* Harper Collins.*

Hurnard, Hannah. *Hind's Feet on High Places.* Living Books.

Hybels, Bill and Wilkins, Rob. *Tender Love.* Moody Press.

Smalley, Gary and Trent, John, Ph.D. *The Language of Love.* Focus on the Family Publishing.

Warren, Neil Clark, Ph.D. *Finding the Love of Your Life.* Focus on the Family Publishing.

Wilson, P.B. *Knight in Shining Armor.* Harvest House Publishers.

---

* Entries marked with asterisks are secular books with tremendous insights. However, the advice in these books needs to be considered in light of God's Word.

Study Guide

1

Taking Inventory

❧

He who disdains instruction despises his own soul, but he who
heeds rebuke gets understanding (Proverbs 15:32).

We can all go out in a blaze of glory but miserable and alone while singing,
"I Did It My Way," or we can choose to take stock of where we presently stand,
review comments and wise counsel, and make a change to improve who we
are. Though we know some blessings are by grace, we must take responsibility
for those that are conditional. Acquiring relationship skills is our responsibility. Renewing our minds is the first step to a transformed life.

She has not obeyed His voice, she has not received correction;
she has not trusted in the LORD, she has not drawn near to her
God (Zephaniah 3:2).

What is the root cause for refusing correction?

1. Take stock of comments you have heard concerning your relationships
   with men and write them out. What is the common thread that keeps
   repeating itself? This is the first hint to where you should focus your
   efforts for renewing your mind.

2. Now find Scriptures that apply to this area of criticism. What does God
   say about the way to handle your situation or attitude?

3. Confess this area of weakness to God. Select a Scripture to memorize
   that will assist you in overcoming and give you a base to stand on.

4. Ask God to select someone who has a successful relationship to be your
   emotional mentor.

5. Read *Hinds' Feet on High Places* by Hannah Hurnard.

6. Ask God to reveal what fears cause you to take destructive courses of action in relationships.

7. Map out your course for healing utilizing Scripture.

8. Begin a journal to record your steps toward preparing your heart for giving and receiving love.

2

Seeing Love for What It Is

Then she said to him, "How can you say, 'I love you,' when your heart is not with me?" (Judges 16:15).

Because of our longing for relationship we are often quick to accept love crumbs from a man's table. Knowing the attributes and behavioral patterns of true love helps us to be more discerning. Choosing to be honest with ourselves even when it hurts is the only safeguard against repeatedly being a victim in romantic relationships. Being established in God's design for love makes us whole individuals who no longer need to be rescued. We are free to see clearly and choose wisely in the affairs of the heart.

I love the LORD, because He has heard my voice and my supplications (Psalm 116:1).

Many waters cannot quench love, nor can the floods drown it. If a man would give for love all the wealth of his house, it would be utterly despised (Song of Solomon 8:7).

Greater love has no one than this, than to lay down one's life for his friends (John 15:13).

What is the outstanding feature of love?

1. What types of behavior and attitudes have you accepted as love from men? Does your list line up with God's idea of love?

2. What makes you settle for less than God's original design for how you should be treated? Are your insecurities and fears based on concrete evidence or emotions?

3. What is the difference between your relationships with women and men? What expectations do you have for both? Why?

4. How would you describe your love relationship with the Lord?

5. What traits would you like to see in your mate? Does the Lord line up with and fulfill your list? Where has He come through when others failed?

6. What tangible steps can you take to solidify a love life with the Lord? Make a list.

3

Setting Safe Boundaries

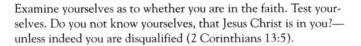

Examine yourselves as to whether you are in the faith. Test yourselves. Do you not know yourselves, that Jesus Christ is in you?—unless indeed you are disqualified (2 Corinthians 13:5).

Being honest with yourself is most of the battle when it comes to overcoming in any situation. Transparency is the best dispeller of secrets and the questionable situations they get us into. Accountability also is the silent guard that keeps us within safe boundaries. Once again, the responsibility to keep ourselves pure is entirely ours—and this does not happen without taking definite steps.

There is a difference between a wife and a virgin. The unmarried woman cares about the things of the Lord, that she may be holy both in body and in spirit...(1 Corinthians 7:34).

Let us search out and examine our ways, and turn back to the
LORD (Lamentations 3:40).

What is the key to overcoming temptation?

1. What are situations and places that set you up for compromising your
sexual purity?

2. What should you do to avoid temptation?

3. Is there anyone from past relationships that you have trouble resisting?
Pray for soul ties with these individuals to be broken.

4. What things cause you difficulty in the area of controlling your sexual
desires—emotionally, physically, and spiritually?

5. What are realistic measures you can take to avoid falling when confronted with the above-mentioned issues?

6. How can you renew your mind to focus on things that keep firm your
resolve to be pure?

7. Establish accountability in a close relationship.

4

Renewing the Mind

❧

And do not be conformed to this world, but be transformed by
the renewing of your mind, that you may prove what is that good
and acceptable and perfect will of God (Romans 12:2).

Separating fact from fiction begins with setting our thoughts in order.
We will become slaves to whatever we think about; therefore, it is of utmost
importance to take dominion over our thought lives. Remember that the
members of your body are subject to you. Just as you chart the direction for
your feet, you must select the subject matter for your mind, realizing that your
heart is the most powerful form of subliminal advertising you will ever

encounter. If you think a McDonald's commercial can make you hungry, just give the mind free rein and see what happens!

For as he thinks in his heart, so is he (Proverbs 23:7).

Finally, brethren, whatever things are true, whatever things are noble, whatever things are just, whatever things are pure, whatever things are lovely, whatever things are of good report, if there is any virtue, and if there is anything praiseworthy—meditate on these things (Philippians 4:8).

What is the key to taking dominion over your actions?

1. What negative issues and relationships from your past color your present attitude? Have you surrendered them to God in exchange for His forgiveness and His healing?

2. What recurring thoughts cause you to be vulnerable in situations that could lead to compromising your personal standards?

3. What do you think of yourself as a woman? What do you deserve according to yourself? According to God?

4. What stops you from feeling you deserve God's best for your life and relationships?

5. Search the Scriptures for God's view of your issues. Write a list of new declarations for yourself to memorize and confess.

5

Keeping Your Heart

Keep your heart with all diligence, for out of it spring the issues of life (Proverbs 4:23).

Our hearts harbor many things that cause us to take unwise action. Our expectations and desires can overwhelm us and color our vision. As we yield to God's direction and timing, the demands of the heart grow more faint. It is in resting in God and releasing all that we long for to Him that the desires of our hearts are finally met.

> For where your treasure is, there your heart will be also (Luke 12:34).

> Hear, my son, and be wise; and guide your heart in the way (Proverbs 23:19).

> He who keeps His command will experience nothing harmful; and a wise man's heart discerns both time and judgment (Ecclesiastes 8:5).

How do we make our hearts subject to us?

1. How do overwhelming desires short circuit our ability to make wise decisions?

2. Dating is for collecting data. What happens if your heart ignores the information gathered?

3. Write a list of your expectations for the man's role in your life. What does God expect? Are you settling for less?

4. What unrealistic expectations do you have about relationships?

5. What do you expect from God in the relationship area? What do you think He expects from you?

6. What part does obeying the Word play in helping you keep your heart in the right place?

7. What area does trust play in your obedience to God?

6

Relax, Relate, Release

❧

Trust in the LORD, and do good; dwell in the land, and feed on
His faithfulness. Delight yourself also in the LORD, and He shall
give you the desires of your heart (Psalm 37:3,4).

God will not share His glory with another—and that includes your potential mate. Until marriage is no longer an idol in your life, the struggle for love
will be a painful one. As we release our desires into God's hands and await
His instruction for our lives, we will lack the fulfillment we so fervently seek.
Stop asking, "Why am I alone?" and begin to ask Him, "Why am I here?" As
you set about fulfilling your purpose in life, the one that you have been crafted
to partner with will be drawn to you.

For you have need of endurance, so that after you have done the
will of God, you may receive the promise: "For yet a little while,
and He who is coming will come and will not tarry" (Hebrews
10:36,37).

How does impatience affect the way we make choices?

1. Have you torn down the idol of marriage in your life? What stops you
   from releasing this area of your life to God?

2. What do you think will happen if you release your desire for marriage to
   God? Why?

3. On a scale of 1 to 10, where would you say your trust level for God is?
   What affects your trust for Him? How can your trust be strengthened?

4. Have you come to a clear understanding of God's purpose for your life?
   How do you presently use your gifts to bless others?

5. How much of your time is spent on activities to nurture yourself versus
   helping others? How can you adjust this balance?

6. Make of list of what concrete steps you can take that will release you to live a more fulfilling life until your mate comes along.

7

Fruit Inspection

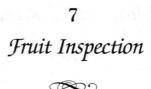

Charm is deceitful and beauty is passing, but a woman who fears the LORD, she shall be praised (Proverbs 31:30).

It is evident that external beauty only lasts so long, and we cannot place our trust on things that change. We need the constant of a spirit that draws others to it because of its goodness and the light it carries—the light of Christ. As you prepare yourself for your mate, also look for the fruit of the Spirit to be evident in the lives of the men you meet.

But the fruit of the Spirit is love, joy, peace, longsuffering, kindness, goodness, faithfulness (Galatians 5:22).

For the fruit of the Spirit is in all goodness, righteousness, and truth (Ephesians 5:9).

Why is fruit important in the life of a believer?

1. Which fruits are a little sour in your garden? Why? What factors affect your fruit? How can this be fixed?

2. How would you evaluate your beauty physically, spiritually, and emotionally? Which areas need improvement? Map out a plan to change.

3. What makes others attractive to you inwardly? Outwardly? Do you possess these same qualities?

4. Do a word search on the words *beauty*, *beautiful*, and *lovely* in the Scriptures. What is God's definition of beautiful?

5. What steps can you take to redefine beauty in your own mind?

6. What steps will you take to become God's definition of beautiful?

7. What do you have to offer to your mate if he were to appear now?

8. How does God's definition of beauty affect what you will look for in a mate?

8

Breaking the Cycle

Brethren, I do not count myself to have apprehended; but one thing I do, forgetting those things which are behind and reaching forward to those things which are ahead (Philippians 3:13).

Remaining bound in bad habits does not free us for the new life God has prepared for us. Because He has furnished us with everything pertaining to life and godliness, it is up to us to honestly evaluate repeat cycles in our lives, draw honest conclusions, and then make purposeful steps to break those patterns with the guidance of the Holy Spirit.

But he who looks into the perfect law of liberty and continues in it, and is not a forgetful hearer but a doer of the work, this one will be blessed in what [she] does (James 1:25).

What is the major key to gaining liberty in our lives?

1. What repeat cycles in your relationships are you aware of?

2. What traits repeatedly crop up in the men you are attracted to?

3. Why are you attracted to this type of man? What does this type of person fulfill in you?

4. If you are what you attract, are there changes needed in your own life? Your perspective? Your way of doing things?

5. How does your mother and sister handle male/female relationships? Is there any similarity in your own life?

6. How does the Word of God say you should conduct your relationships? Does His Word match what is presently happening in your life? What thought processes need to change? What self-esteem issues need to be dealt with?

7. Write down the cycles that need to be broken in your relationships. Prayerfully seek God for keys to healing in this area. Write a plan for the steps you will take toward freedom.

9

Unraveling Generational Behavior

The soul who sins shall die. The son shall not bear the guilt of the father, nor the father bear the guilt of the son. The righteousness of the righteous shall be upon himself, and the wickedness of the wicked shall be upon himself (Ezekiel 18:20).

Well, mama did it—and her mama did it—doesn't necessarily mean that you have to do it. Especially if it bears little or no good out of it. As Christians we are called to a higher dimension of living. We are to no longer seek what the flesh was taught, but what we discern by the spirit, based on our heavenly Father's Word.

That you may be sons [and daughters] of your Father in heaven; for He makes His sun rise on the evil and on the good, and sends rain on the just and on the unjust (Matthew 5:45).

Therefore you shall be perfect, just as your Father in heaven is perfect (Matthew 5:48).

Where do we inherit our true character traits now that we are believers?

1. What do you see in your mother that you don't like?

2. Do you harbor resentment toward your mother for the things you don't like in her behavior? What needs to take place in order to release forgiveness?

3. What do you catch yourself doing just like she does? Which similar attitudes exist? Why?

4. What do you need to do to break the cycle of repeated generational mistakes in your own life?

5. What has to take place in order for your life to be transformed?

6. Why is renewing the mind through the Word of God important?

7. What steps will you take to get rid of "stinkin' thinkin' "? Chart out a daily devotional plan for yourself.

10

Let's Get Real

⤫⤬⤫

Do not be wise in your own eyes; fear the LORD and depart from evil (Proverbs 3:7).

The way of a fool is right in his own eyes, but he who heeds counsel is wise (Proverbs 12:15).

Love is blind they say, and yet it shouldn't be. God loves us with His eyes wide open. We get to choose if we want Him to love us close up, or love us from afar. Even God has His limits as to what He will tolerate in His presence. We are precious vessels that belong to Him. It is an insult to God when we allow ourselves to remain in relationships that rob us of the peace and wholeness that He desires for us. He recognizes our value, others should too.

Do not be unequally yoked together with unbelievers. For what fellowship has righteousness with lawlessness? And what communion has light with darkness? (2 Corinthians 6:14).

Do not give what is holy to the dogs; nor cast your pearls before swine, lest they trample them under their feet, and turn and tear you in pieces (Matthew 7:6).

How do we leave ourselves open to having our hearts abused? What is God's first requirement for the man in your life?

1. Review the story of Samson in Judges 14. What was Samson's first mistake? Can you see yourself in his story?

2. What happens to our discernment when our flesh gets in the way?

3. Why is taking heed to the counsel of others who love you important?

4. Are you making excuses for the behavior of someone in your life? Why?

5. Does the person in your life draw you closer to God or cause you to compromise your faith? Does he bring out the best in you? Encourage you to utilize your gifts? Make an honest assessment of your relationship. Ask God to give you clarity.

11

The Beauty Makeover

Charm is deceitful and beauty is passing, but a woman who fears the LORD, she shall be praised (Proverbs 31:30).

Do not let your adornment be merely outward—arranging the
hair, wearing gold, or putting on fine apparel—rather let it be the
hidden beauty of a gentle and quiet spirit, which is very precious
in the sight of God (1 Peter 3:3,4).

"Pretty is as pretty does" goes the saying, and I think God agrees. Though
men are moved by what they see, they stay because of what they experience
with you. Make sure your beauty makeover goes beyond the surface; make sure
your regimen includes work from the inside out.

How beautiful upon the mountains are the feet of him who brings
good news, who proclaims peace, who brings glad tidings of good
things, who proclaims salvation, who says to Zion, "Your God
reigns!" (Isaiah 52:7).

**What type of people are always a welcome sight to you? How do they
make you feel?**

1. Do a complete evaluation of yourself from the inside out—physically,
   emotionally, and spiritually.

2. What work do you need to do on your physical appearance? List your
   goals, then plot out steps toward achieving your goal.

3. What work needs to take place emotionally? What areas need to be
   healed? What issues need to be settled?

4. Honestly evaluate your relationship with God. Are you in love with
   Him? What needs to take place to bring you to a deeper intimacy with
   Him? Make a commitment to a devotional time, and make plans for that
   time with Him.

5. What needs to take place in your life in order for you to see yourself as
   God sees you? To get to the place of peaceful self-acceptance? Write a
   confession about yourself based on the Word of God.

12

Mastering the Art of Housekeeping

Now therefore, thus says the LORD of hosts: Consider your ways!
(Haggai 1:5).

Prepare your outside work, make it fit for yourself in the field; and
afterward build your house (Proverbs 24:27).

A friend of mine told me once a man wants three things: to be well fed,
well loved (in the physical sense), and well appreciated. In return you will be
well loved, well kept, and well satisfied. Every woman should know how to
make her home an oasis for her man and for herself. This is why establishing
good housekeeping and instilling good habits in that area should begin now.
It is also important to know that good housekeeping is not just physical; it is
spiritual as well. Begin today to get your physical and spiritual house in order.

Who can find a virtuous wife? For her worth is far above rubies
(Proverbs 31:10).

**List the virtuous wife's credentials that match your own. Where do you
need work?**

1. List the areas of housekeeping in Proverbs 31: within the house; outside
   the house; within her spirit; within the occupants of her household.

2. Make a list of the "houses" in your life that need attention. What is your
   game plan for getting God's "Housekeeping Seal of Approval"?

3. What areas do you need to work on in your physical house? Make a fun
   plan for redecorating.

4. Now make a list of the people whose lives you can "decorate" with love.
   Plan a special surprise that comes from your heart.

5. What special thing can you do for yourself that will make you an oasis for
   others?

13

The Art of Conversation

A foolish woman is clamorous: She is simple, and knows nothing (Proverbs 9:13).

It is better to dwell in a corner of a housetop, than in a house with a contentious woman (Proverbs 25:24).

"Less is more," so we hear. True conversation far surpasses the spoken word. It is also a life led well in front of those we want to affect. Our everyday example affects people more than anything we can say. Living, listening, leaning on God—these are the three steps to effective conversation.

A soft answer turns away wrath, but a harsh word stirs up anger (Proverbs 15:1).

How does a quiet spirit prepare the heart of someone so they will receive what you have to say?

1. Read the book of Esther. What were the steps Esther took in order to present her case to the king?

2. Who did Esther submit her plea to first?

3. What did she do to prepare the heart of the king for what she had to say?

4. What was her posture when she told what she needed? What was her attitude?

5. How crucial is timing to the process of communication?

6. What part does God play when we need someone to really hear us?

7. How important is prayer when we anticipate confronting important issues with those we love? Why?

8. How do we ensure that we leave enough room for our loved ones to hear the Holy Spirit?

14

Mastering Submission

> Wives, submit to your own husbands, as to the Lord (Ephesians 5:22).

> Wives, likewise, be submissive to your own husbands, that even if some do not obey the word, they, without a word, may be won by the conduct of their wives, when they observe your chaste conduct accompanied by fear (1 Peter 3:1,2).

Everything in God's kingdom seems to be opposite to the way of the world. In God's economy you give to get, you forgive your enemies, you humble yourself in order to be lifted up. *Every* Christian is called to submit, whether male or female. As we learn to yield to one another we discover the true source of power and liberation.

> Rather let it be the hidden person of the heart, with the incorruptible beauty of a gentle and quiet spirit, which is very precious in the sight of God. For in this manner, in former times, the holy women who trusted in God also adorned themselves, being submissive to their own husbands, as Sarah obeyed Abraham, calling him lord, whose daughters you are if you do good and are not afraid with any terror (1 Peter 3:4-6).

What gives us the confidence to submit to those in authority?

1. Why does God call us to submit?

2. Who is ultimately in charge of our lives? Of those in authority over us?

3. What causes you to struggle with the word *submission*? What preconceived notions do you have of what that means?

4. What happens when we don't submit to authority?

5. How does God use those in authority over us in our lives?

6. What does submission ultimately achieve in our lives?

15

Tearing Down the Idols

❧

You shall have no other gods before Me (Exodus 20:3).

Do not go after other gods to serve them and worship them, and do not provoke Me to anger with the works of your hands; and I will not harm you (Jeremiah 25:6).

God is a jealous God and well He should be. You heart is a small thing to ask for in exchange for the life of His Son. Anything other than Christ that becomes a fixation in our lives stands between us and God. The all-consuming desire for a mate can become an idol, robbing us of the peace and joy God desires for us. We need to have the right perspective. As we open our arms and embrace God completely, seeking Him first above all things, He in turn sends physical arms to hug us back.

For where your treasure is, there your heart will be also (Luke 12:34).

But seek first the kingdom of God and His righteousness, and all these things shall be added to you (Matthew 6:33).

What is the key to getting the desires of your heart?

1. Make an honest assessment of what is most important to you.

2. How much of your time is spent worrying about your prospects for marriage? How much time is spent talking with friends on this subject?

3. How much time do you spend cultivating your relationship with God? Are you in love with Him?

4. Have you bargained with God when it comes to your heart? Are you waiting to give Him your all after you get married?

5. Is your heart divided between your longing for a husband and fulfilling the call God has on your life? Why?

6. Do you think God can trust you with a husband right now? Why?

7. Who would win the contest for your affections right now?

"A Final Word"
Time to Celebrate

So he answered and said, "You shall love the LORD your God with all your heart, with all your soul, with all your strength, and with all your mind," and "your neighbor as yourself" (Luke 10:27).

There is a difference between a wife and a virgin. The unmarried woman cares about the things of the Lord, that she may be holy both in body and in spirit. But she who is married cares about the things of the world—how she may please her husband (1 Corinthians 7:34).

The only one who can love us—truly love us the way we desire to be loved—is the Lord. As we draw close to Him we will find our fulfillment. Our love for the Lord will become contagious, spilling out to all we encounter. As we love those who are available to be loved in our world right now, love visits us in bountiful measure, filling all the empty places in our lives. It is in the glow of living a complete life that others are drawn to us. Why? Because we're in love! And love attracts love.

> Delight yourself also in the LORD, and He shall give you the desires of your heart (Psalm 37:4).

What opens God's hands to grant us all that we crave?

1. In what areas have you put your life on hold? Why?

2. What areas or circumstances in your life do you feel having a husband would help? Can God address those areas right now?

3. Are you actively pursuing God's plan for you? Are you taking full advantage of opportunities presented to you now? Why or why not?

4. What can you do to extend your love to someone today? Who can you help right now? Is there a child you can invest in right now?

5. Make a list of places you'd like to go, things you'd like to see, and skills you'd like to learn. Select one, and get started on making it happen.

6. Write a commitment to yourself and to God to take advantage of your life as it is now. Make a list of what you intend to do to make that happen.

7. Choose a blessing to celebrate today.

Books by
Michelle McKinney Hammond

101 Ways to Get and Keep His Attention
The DIVA Principle®
The DIVA Principle®—A Sister Girl's Guide
Ending the Search for Mr. Right
Finding the Right Woman for You
Get Over It and On With It
How to Be Blessed and Highly Favored
If Men Are Like Buses, Then How Do I Catch One?
In Search of the Proverbs 31 Man
The Power of Being a Woman
Prayer Guide for the Brokenhearted
Sassy Girl's Guide to Loving God
Sassy, Single, & Satisfied
Secrets of an Irresistible Woman
Unveiling the DIVA Mystique
What Becomes of the Brokenhearted?
What to Do Until Love Finds You
Where Are You, God?
Why Do I Say "Yes" When I Need To Say "No?"

Direct all correspondence and inquiries to:

HeartWing Ministries
c/o Michelle McKinney-Hammond
P.O. Box 11052
Chicago, IL 60611

heartwing@yahoo.com
www.michellehammond.com

Other Good
Harvest House Reading

YOUR KNIGHT IN SHINING ARMOR
by *P.B. Wilson*
Breaking the holding pattern faced by many who are waiting for
their life partners, Wilson helps you become complete as a single,
so you can bring *all* of your resources into marriage with joyful and
realistic expectations.

FINDING YOUR PERFECT MATE
by *H. Norman Wright*
Thoughtful words of wisdom and encouragement on one of life's
most important turning points. Dynamic insights based on years of
premarital counseling for people seeksing God's guidance in finding
a perfect lifetime companion.

HOW CAN I BE SURE?
by *Bob Phillips*
A premarriage inventory especially for use with young couples who
are contemplating marriage. You'll explore one another's thoughts
and feelings and find areas of agreement and a basis for resolving
disagreements.

BEFORE YOU SAY "I DO"®
by *H. Norman Wright*
This creative resource for premarital preparation is packed with
Scripture references, personality tests, goal-setting guides, and many
other effective items to help build a firm foundation for a future
together.